The Making of *Go Down, Moses*

The Making
of
Go Down, Moses

JAMES EARLY

SOUTHERN METHODIST UNIVERSITY PRESS • DALLAS

©1972 • Southern Methodist University Press • Dallas

Library of Congress Catalog Card Number: 72-80404

ISBN Number: 0-87074-003-2

CONTENTS

PREFACE

TWENTY-FIVE YEARS AGO Robert Penn Warren spoke of the interpretation of Faulkner's works as the most challenging single task for critics in modern American literature. Warren's invitation has been accepted with enthusiasm. Faulkner, who had slight affection for criticism or for critics, has recently been the object of more critical attention than any other twentieth-century writer in English, with the possible exception of Joyce. Roughly twice as many studies are now devoted to Faulkner as to Eliot and Hemingway, his closest rivals among modern American writers in scholarly popularity. The plenitude of recent books includes *Crowell's Handbook of Faulkner*, *A Faulkner Glossary*, *Who's Who in Faulkner*, *Faulkner's People*, and *Faulkner's Library: A Catalog*.

Apart from a generally useful continuation of the study of style and technique inaugurated by Conrad Aiken and Warren Beck, certain trends have been notable in the American criticism of Faulkner. Aubrey Starke, George Marion O'Donnell, Malcolm Cowley, Warren, and others of the most perceptive of Faulkner's early champions emphasized his sociology—his creation of a mythical kingdom in north Mississippi founded by heroic Sartorises and Sutpens, inhabited by enduring blacks and country people, and taken over by invading Snopeses. In his great essay published in the *New Republic* in 1946, Warren suggested lines for future investigation, among them Faulkner's use of "polarities, oppositions, paradoxes, inversions of roles"; images of the hunt and of flight; images of compulsion and of freedom; the symbolic relationship between man and the earth; and "the device . . . we might call the frozen moment." In following the hints of Warren and the readings of French writers such as André Malraux and Jean-Paul Sartre, later critics seemed particularly concerned with uncovering archetypal patterns in Faulkner's fiction, with exploring the use of myth and allegory. More recently, in the wake of the celebrated Stockholm address, there have been efforts to find beneath the formal complexities of Faulkner's works a simple ethical message. In place of the nihilistic cultural psychotic discovered by Maxwell Geismar, or the tortured existentialist conceived by critics under the spell of the French, a quite different figure has begun to emerge—most prominently in the work of Cleanth Brooks—the Christian moralist, the defender of traditional community values.

This brief summary of over twenty years' critical effort suggests that Faulkner's critics have found in his books very much what they brought to them, and that the writings are rich enough to be read in diverse ways and on several levels. Perceptive and helpful as many of Faulkner's critics have been, a great deal of the criticism has been unsatisfactory because of distortions arising from the forcing of intellectual presuppositions upon the works. A common source of these distortions has been the critics' impatience with mere story and mere characters. Simple fictional creation has not interested those preoccupied with underlying myths; merely human relationships have seemed trivial to those fascinated with allegorical schemes. Critics have been too ready to slash through the living flesh of Faulkner's fictions to slice out veins of abstract meaning. It has sometimes seemed that only what could be intellectualized was considered worthy of critical attention.

Faulkner is above all a master storyteller, and it is salutary to recall his insistence that the varied symbolic patterns he employed were only his means for telling his stories, selected, he loved to say,

as a carpenter selects his tools and his planks for a building. For
Faulkner the center of his completed edifice was in the characters.
He repeatedly declared in seemingly old-fashioned words that his
essential concern was "to create believable people in credible moving situations in the most moving way" he could; once in a *Paris
Review* interview he stated to Jean Stein—hyperbolically, to be sure
—that "there's always a point in the book where the characters
themselves rise up and take charge and finish" it. Faulkner's characters are seldom entirely believable in the way the characters of
Jane Austen, Tolstoy, or George Eliot are believable. Most discerning readers would agree, I am certain, that Faulkner demon-
strates his genius primarily as a narrator, a creator of overwhelm-
ingly moving situations, rather than as a creator of notably credible
people. Yet, in the highly charged situations in which they are
placed, Faulkner's people take on for us an almost overpowering
reality. Joe Christmas and Isaac McCaslin may be far less individu-
alized in their inner consciousness than Emma Woodhouse, Natasha
Rostov, or Dorothea Brooke, but when Joe curses God from the
pulpit of a Negro church or when Isaac learns from the plantation
ledgers about his grandfather's philandering with his slaves, we
respond powerfully to their inner selves. Much of Faulkner's great-
ness as a novelist has its source in his power of illusion. He compels
us to believe in the reality of his characters' moral lives—even though
his characters are foreshortened to fit the particular perspectives
created by his various modes of narration.

There are a great number of encyclopedic accounts of Faulkner's writings but very few book-length studies of individual novels,
and no really comprehensive investigations of the genesis of any of
his works. In this study of *Go Down, Moses*, I have considered in
depth a work of particular importance in Faulkner's career, and I
have attempted to give a full account of the workings of Faulkner's
creative imagination. I have been especially concerned with the
gradual development of his themes, his verbal and narrative tech-
niques, and his conception of his characters between the germina-
tion of what became *Go Down, Moses* in hunting stories of 1934 and
1935 and the publication of his saga of the McCaslin family in
1942. My study is based upon close readings of both the published
magazine versions of several of the stories included in the book and

the unpublished typescripts in Faulkner's own collection preserved in the Alderman Library of the University of Virginia. Although my method is largely genetic, my intention is critical. Genetic study is no substitute for careful reading of the final text. It has its own particular emphases, and it can produce a distorted view of the finished work. Yet for a book as difficult, as ambiguous, and as fragmentary as *Go Down, Moses* it is an immense aid to critical understanding.

My work was originally stimulated by William Van O'Connor's pioneering essay in genetic criticism, "The Wilderness Theme in Faulkner's 'The Bear,'" *Accent* (first published in Winter 1953) and later incorporated in revised form in *The Tangled Fire of William Faulkner*. I profited from a discussion with Stanley Sultan, whose view of *Go Down, Moses* is expressed in "Call Me Ishmael: The Hagiography of Isaac McCaslin," *Texas Studies in Language and Literature* (Spring 1961). An interesting but, I believe, misguided essay very critical of Faulkner's elaboration of the magazine versions of his stories is Marvin Klotz's "Procrustean Revision in Faulkner's *Go Down, Moses*," in *American Literature* (March 1965). Michael Millgate's *The Achievement of William Faulkner* (New York, 1966), the most useful general study of Faulkner's career and writings, contains an excellent brief account of *Go Down, Moses*, but one which seriously overestimates the aesthetic unity achieved by Faulkner in that work. I have profited from the scholarship of James B. Meriwether, especially from his bibliographical study, *The Literary Career of William Faulkner* (Princeton, 1961).

The late John Cook Wyllie and the William Faulkner Foundation kindly allowed me to read the manuscript materials in the Alderman Library. I wish to thank Faulkner's daughter, Mrs. Paul D. Summers, Jr., for granting me permission to publish excerpts from that material. A Shell Oil Company grant from Vassar College made it possible for me to visit Charlottesville, and David Coldwell and the Graduate Council of the Humanities at Southern Methodist University provided time and funds for the completion of this book.

JAMES EARLY

Dallas, Texas
February 29, 1972

PART ONE

The Original Stories

CHAPTER ONE

LUCAS BEAUCHAMP

AT LEAST since Malcolm Cowley included it in his *Portable Faulkner* in 1946, "The Bear" has been regarded as one of Faulkner's greatest achievements. The book of which "The Bear" is a part has been judged with much less certainty. Some of the uncertainty has grown out of the question of the book's genre. Is it a novel, as Faulkner insisted in his conferences with students at the University of Virginia; or is it, as the original title *Go Down, Moses and Other Stories* suggested,[1] a collection of loosely related stories? A number of the critical studies of Faulkner's novels have omitted it, and the book retains discrepancies and unsettling shifts of tone stemming from its origin in a group of relatively simple, independently conceived stories published in various magazines between 1935 and 1942.

Go Down, Moses is both greater and less than the most famous of its parts, "The Bear." Published six years after *Absalom, Absalom!*, it lacks the organic unity of that novel or even a unity comparable to that of its immediate predecessor, *The Hamlet*, which is startlingly various. In 1941 and 1942 Faulkner seemed no longer capable of finding a form for his McCaslin chronicle comparable to that which made the story of the Sutpens so overpowering in his *Absalom, Absalom!* of 1936. Yet to read "The Bear" apart from its context amid the other McCaslin stories of *Go Down, Moses* is to misread it. "The Bear" was the last of the McCaslin stories written; it grew gradually out of the others, and its meaning is apparent only when it is read with them. The fourth section, constituting half of the story's length, is, as Faulkner insisted, fully comprehensible only in relation to the whole volume,[2] and the magnificent concluding section of "The Bear," though followed by two other stories, is a wonderfully fitting culmination to the entire volume. Despite its fragmentary nature, *Go Down, Moses* is more impressive in its totality than any of its parts. And it provides—to some degree because it is fragmentary—an almost unique opportunity to study Faulkner's creative activity. Because of the scarcity of surviving evidence of revisions and also because of their aesthetic wholeness *The Sound and the Fury, As I Lay Dying,*[3] and *Absalom, Absalom!* reveal less of the shaping actions of Faulkner's creative imagination than the less satisfactorily unified *Go Down, Moses.* This book contains both examples of abortive efforts to achieve aesthetic unity and, in "The Bear" and to a lesser extent in "Delta Autumn," supreme achievements of Faulkner's synthesizing imagination.

By 1940, when Faulkner was writing early versions of several of the stories he would later include in *Go Down, Moses*, his period of greatest creativity was several years behind him. He had written five major novels between 1928 and 1932—*Sartoris, The Sound and the Fury, As I Lay Dying, Sanctuary,* and *Light in August*—and more than forty stories. These included many of his best shorter pieces, among them "Red Leaves," "A Rose for Emily," "A Justice," and "That Evening Sun." In addition to the great independent stories, he wrote in these years a number of things such as "Spotted Horses" and "The Hound" which were later to be incorporated into the novels about the Snopes family.

In May, 1933, Faulkner began a year's service as screenwriter for M-G-M and then, after eighteen months off, returned to work almost two years for Twentieth Century Fox before his contract expired in August, 1937. At the beginning of this period of screenwriting Faulkner's fictional output fell off only slightly. Despite his obligations to M-G-M, he wrote "Wash" and "A Bear Hunt" in the last months of 1933. "Wash" was the germ of *Absalom, Absalom!* "A Bear Hunt," the first of Faulkner's stories abount hunters, is really concerned with a hoax instead of a hunt. But it contains the earliest description of the bottomland, thickly tangled with vegetation, on which the great hunting stories would be placed; and it introduces Ash, the Negro camp cook, and, in minor roles, Major de Spain, the owner of the hunting camp,[4] as well as an old man, Uncle Ike McCaslin, who would later be transformed into the youthful hero of "The Bear."

The time between movie contracts was fruitful. Faulkner wrote *Pylon,* published in March 1935, and was already concerned with *Absalom, Absalom!,* his major work of the middle thirties. In addition, four of the Civil War stories later included in *The Unvanquished* were published in 1934 and 1935, and others may have been conceived in these years. In connection with *Go Down, Moses,* the most important work of the period was "Lion," a story published in the December 1935 issue of *Harper's.* This is Faulkner's earliest account of the great hunt, of the immense dog Lion's fatal pursuit of Old Ben, the bear, and of the dog's brave and childish admirer, Boon Hogganbeck.

In the summer of 1940 Faulkner was forty-two years old and had been back from California nearly three years. The first two years back in Oxford were, for Faulkner, notably unproductive. At least a book a year had been published since 1929, but only one story appeared in 1937. *The Unvanquished* came out in the following year, but of its seven chapters only one was wholly new. In 1939 Faulkner published in a single volume with alternating chapters two short novels, "The Wild Palms" and "The Old Man." Much of that year was spent on the doings of the Snopes family, filling out and shaping material Faulkner had been mulling over in his imagination since the twenties. The result was the loose and sprawling, extravagant and brilliant novel, *The Hamlet,* and a preliminary story, "Barn Burning."

After finishing *The Hamlet,* Faulkner turned to shorter fiction, publishing more stories in 1940 than in any year after 1934. Four of these stories were later revised to become part of *Go Down, Moses.*

Two other stories incorporated in that book were written in 1940 and published later. These were the title story, which came out in *Colliers* in January 1941, and the introductory story, "Was," which was withheld until the book appeared in 1942. The first of the pieces published in 1940 was "A Point of Law," in the June 22 *Colliers*. *Harper's* included "The Old People" in September and "Pantaloon in Black" in October. A sequel to "A Point of Law" entitled "Gold Is Not Always" was in the November *Atlantic.*

"A Point of Law," which after substantial alteration and expansion became the first chapter of the second section of *Go Down, Moses*, entitled "The Fire and the Hearth," must have seemed to casual readers of *Colliers* a conventional piece of dialect fiction dealing with comical southern Negroes. In tone the story differed only slightly from some that Faulkner's brother John, far more sympathetic to the Mississippi racial status quo than William, published in the same magazine.[5] The Negro protagonist, Lucas Beauchamp, pictured in William Meade Prince's illustrations as resembling an aging Louis Armstrong, was a crafty but on the whole likable sharecropper who became entangled in his own trickery in betraying to the sheriff and his men a rival moonshiner with whom his daughter was in love. The daughter made sure that he was incriminated along with his prospective son-in-law. After "Luke" agreed to pay for improvements in the younger man's house in order to persuade his daughter to marry so that all potential witnesses would be members of the same family and therefore unable to give valid testimony against each other in court, Luke's daughter disclosed that she had been secretly married all along. At the end of the story the son-in-law has spent the money intended for domestic improvements on another still and placed himself under Lucas's direction, only to have Lucas refuse to help him explain to his bride what he has done with the cash. In the sequel, "Gold Is Not Always," which formed the basis of the second chapter of "The Fire and the Hearth," Lucas was involved in a search for buried treasure. He duped a white salesman of a metal-detecting device into giving him the machine by planting silver dollars for the salesman to find, thus arousing his greed for the treasure, which he believed Lucas would help him locate. This episode recalls the manner in which Flem Snopes's story concluded, with Lucas telling his white landlord, Carothers Edmonds, how he had rented the machine to the salesman for twenty-five dollars a night for several nights until he finally "got shut of him."

Little in the magazine versions of these stories suggests serious concern with the harsher realities of Negro life in the South. The imagination which had conceived Joe Christmas and Charles Etienne St. Valery Bon seemed only partially engaged. For the most part Lucas conformed to a comfortable white stereotype of the Negro, and his wife, as yet given no name, was a shrewish minor figure. But in the course of writing these stories and a third one, unpublished, entitled at first "Apotheosis," then "An Absolution," and finally "The Fire and the Hearth," Faulkner began to move toward a more interesting conception of the characters. Even in "A Point of Law," where Lucas's wife was presented as a shrill complainer, Faulkner mentioned a fire, symbolic of marital fidelity, which had burned on Lucas's hearth continuously for forty-five years. The fire seems unrelated to Faulkner's characterization in the first story, but it becomes of central significance in the third one, which, after additions and changes, became the final chapter of the "Fire and the Hearth" section of *Go Down, Moses*. This story is focused on Molly, the wife, and the troubles caused her by Lucas's mania for finding buried gold. At the last moment the divorce proceedings which Molly had initiated were called off by Lucas, who renounced treasure-hunting and presented her with a nickel sack of candy soft enough for her to "gum."

Molly, who did not appear in "Gold Is Not Always," is a different person in this story from the coarse, complaining wife of "A Point of Law," and Lucas has undergone a more subtle transformation. Originally Lucas and his wife were simply sharecroppers who had been tenants on Edmonds's land for forty-five years. But in working out the third story of the sequence, Faulkner decided to make Lucas a native of the place, born in the lifetime of the Edmonds of the preceding generation. At one time he had Lucas address Carothers as "Master," forgetfully mistaking him for his father. The relationship between Edmonds and the Negroes had been conceived originally as one demonstrating the trials of a short-tempered but essentially benevolent white who was continually put upon by irresponsible and, to his view, incomprehensible black tenants. But as

Faulkner developed the theme of marital fidelity implicit in the enduring hearth fire, he saw that he could present Molly's predicament more effectively if she were viewed through the sympathetic eyes of a white man. In the first of the two typescripts of this third story, which are in the Alderman Library of the University of Virginia, he attempted to make Edmonds's sympathy plausible primarily by modifying his relationship with Lucas. He made Carothers remember the old Negro as the companion of his boyhood, who had been with him when he first learned to ride a horse and, in a way which resembled Sam Fathers's guidance of the young hunter of "The Old People," had followed just behind him when he first went into the field with a gun. But it became apparent that a closer connection with Molly herself was needed to explain Carothers's sympathetic concern. In the margin of the first paragraph of the typescript Faulkner wrote, "Mollie wet nurse & doctor, mother died. High water. Doctor delayed."[6] The second typescript incorporates an account of Molly's delivering Roth and moving into his father's house until he was weaned, leaving her older children in Lucas's care, and it includes a reference to the "tragic complexity" of the white man's motherless childhood which would take on more meaning in Faulkner's later amplification of the story.

The increased intimacy between Carothers Edmonds and the aged Negro woman may reflect something of Faulkner's own feelings for his old "Mammy." Edmonds's age, which increased in various versions from forty to forty-one and then to forty-three, is very close to Faulkner's when he wrote these stories, and Molly's description makes clear her resemblance to Caroline Barr[7] to whom *Go Down, Moses* is dedicated. Callie Barr had gnarled black hands like Molly's hands, which Faulkner described as setting themselves off from her white apron like cramped inksplashes. And Molly's numerous skirts and underskirts seem to have been suggested by Callie's undergarments. After undressing Callie when she was struck by a car toward the end of her approximately hundred years of life, Mrs. Falkner told her sons that she had never seen so many petticoats nor anyone so small and helpless.[8] Caroline Barr Clark had often diverted the young Faulkner with her stories of slave life and of her experiences during the Reconstruction. John Faulkner believed that "it was by the yardstick of his memory of Mammy . . .

that Bill measured integration."[9] William had Callie Barr cared for
in her final years and regularly visited her. When she died in
February of the year these stories were conceived, Faulkner had
her body brought to his house to lie in the living room. He preached
a funeral sermon[10] and had a stone placed over her grave and
inscribed,

"MAMMY"
1840   1940
Her White Children Bless Her
Callie Barr Clark[11]

The transformation of Molly is the most striking development
that occurred during the writing of the three stories, but the modifications in Faulkner's conception of Lucas are as important and as
interesting. From the first, Lucas had a vitality and a complexity of
personality unrelated to the triviality of the events in which he was
involved. His considerable wealth was related to his actions in "A
Point of Law," but his prickly independence and his impenetrable
dignity seemed unnecessary to the plot. It was easy to understand
his assuming the part of "the nigger" when informing on his son-in-
law, wrapping himself in "an aura of patient and impassive stupidity
like a smell almost." But there is much that is superfluous to his
role in the passages describing the impression he made on Carothers
Edmonds as he parried a question about his whiskey still just before
they both rode into Jefferson for the trial. It seemed to the white
man that the face he saw "was absolutely blank, impenetrable. Even
the eyes appeared to have nothing behind them." And Edmonds
"thought and not for the first time in his life. I am not only looking
at a face older than mine . . . , but at a man whose race was pure
ten thousand years when my own anonymous beginnings became
mixed enough to produce me."[12] By the time he wrote "Gold Is Not
Always," Faulkner had a clearer sense of Lucas. There is no more
of his becoming "the nigger"; at the start of the story he is allowed
to prevail over the intentions of the white salesman and is described
as looking over that man "not only with dignity but with command."
Lucas's clothes are described in detail for the first time and, although he is without the threadbare elegance of the mohair trousers

Faulkner would give him in the final version of the story, he is impressive in his "clean, faded overalls," open vest with "a heavy gold watchchain" looped across, and "the thirty-dollar handmade beaver hat" which Edmonds's father had given him.

But a basis for future developments more significant than Lucas's appearance and his formidable bearing toward his white acquaintances lay in Faulkner's use of his point of view as the principal one in telling the stories. Even from the earliest typescript Faulkner led his readers to identify with Lucas as he forced his will upon his white neighbors. He might seem simply an irksome nuisance most of the time to Carothers Edmonds, but to Faulkner's readers he was a fellow human being trying to cope with a recalcitrant world. Faulkner's most perceptive studies of blacks had previously had men of mixed blood as protagonists, and, characteristically, he began to think of Lucas as a mulatto long before he had any idea of relating him to the McCaslin family. A passage crossed out from the typescript of "Gold Is Not Always" at the University of Virginia refers to "his face of a very dark Arab." The first typescript of the third story mentions his "faintly Moorish features," features which became finally, in *Go Down, Moses*, "faintly Syriac," "the color of a used saddle."

CHAPTER TWO

STORIES OF NEGROES
AND STORIES OF HUNTING

THE OTHER STORIES published in 1940 were unlike the light, comic anecdotes of Lucas Beauchamp. In "The Old People," the third of Faulkner's hunting stories, a boy is ritually marked with the blood of his first deer. A second, more powerful sign of his initiation into the moral world of the hunt is his vision of a ghostly, heroic buck, representative of the old people, the Indian fathers of all who follow their paths in the natural wilderness. "Pantaloon in Black" concerns Rider, another black tenant of Carothers Edmonds,[1] who has kept a fire glowing on his family hearth. Perhaps Faulkner conceived this story as a pathetic counterpart of the domestic comedy of Lucas and Molly. It is placed in *Go Down, Moses* between "The Fire and the Hearth" and "The Old People" so as to give Faulkner's reader a sense of the difficulty of being black in a society dominated by whites, reinforcing passages Faulkner interpolated into the early stories portraying life on the tamed land. A black giant, boss of a sawmill gang, buries his wife of six months and on returning home sees her apparition. After she fades from him, he ranges numbly through scenes of violence and of quiet beauty, working, drinking,

11

and striding over moon-drenched countryside until he senses a way
to join his lost love. He exposes the cheating of the white operator
of a crooked dice game in order to provoke his own lynching.
Though marred by the insistent use of a crude Negro dialect which
prevents readers from immersing themselves entirely in the mind of
the stricken husband, the early portions of the story powerfully
convey delicate feelings which are not made explicit but which are
suggested by primitive and violent distracted actions. But in the
concluding section Faulkner abandons subtlety in changing his narration. With heavy-handed irony he tells of the Negro's capture
through a conversation between an obtuse deputy sheriff and his
quarrelsome, party-going wife which concludes with the deputy's
saying that "them damn niggers" might as well be a herd of wild
buffaloes when it comes to natural human feelings.

"Pantaloon in Black" had superficial connections with the Lucas
stories, but "The Old People" had no relationship at all. Told in the
earliest manuscript version by twelve-year-old Quentin Compson,
who also, at the age of sixteen, had been the narrator of "Lion," it
is a principal source of "The Bear" although, unlike "Lion," none of
it was incorporated into the completed story. It brings together
characters from the two earlier hunting stories and Sam Fathers,
the part Indian, former slave narrator of "A Justice," the superb
comic story of Indian and Negro relationships which Faulkner had
published in 1931. Sam, an old man, seemingly impervious to time,
living in the past and wholly superior to the trivial concerns of adult
members of the white race, came ultimately to take a place in *Go
Down, Moses* comparable to that of Lucas—representing in the
wilderness the surviving spirit of the Indian, as Lucas represented
on the tamed land the endurance of the Negro.

The habit of shifting characters from one story to another often
led Faulkner to striking inconsistencies, because the characters seldom remained as they had been created, and the relation between
dates and ages was often erratic. Judging from the dating of inci-
dents in the novel about the Compson family, *The Sound and the
Fury*, "The Old People" takes place a year or two before 1905; yet
the characters are no younger than they were in "A Bear Hunt,"
which took place in the midst of the Depression of the thirties.[2]
Isaac McCaslin, who was to replace Quentin as the central figure

when the story was rewritten for *Go Down, Moses,* appears again
in a minor role as old Uncle Ike. Major de Spain, the owner of the
camp on the Tallahatchie River bottom, is of at least middle age.
He shares the leadership of the hunters with Quentin's father, who
was later to be transformed into Isaac's elder cousin, McCaslin
Edmonds. In "The Old People" the part-Indian ancestry of both
Boon Hogganbeck and Sam Fathers is changed. Boon loses the
grandmother he had in "Lion," the niece of the chief who had
owned the land on which the hunts took place, and, conversely,
Sam's lineage is made more distinguished. Sam has become that
chief's grandson. Still later, when Faulkner wrote "The Bear," he
became the son of that chief, Ikkemotubbe; and his mother, who had
been simply a slave woman, was transformed into a quadroon.
Sam's aloof and dignified bearing toward all white men in "The Old
People" is in keeping with his noble lineage. Sam's age as well as
his ancestry is different. In "A Justice," which apparently took place
a few years before the events of this story when Quentin's grandfather was still alive, he was nearly a hundred years old, but here
he is an ageless seventy. The changes in Faulkner's conception of
Sam Fathers are reflected in the connotations of his name. Originally
he was named Had-Two-Fathers[3] because his mother had an
Indian lover as well as a black husband, but when he was made the
grandson of the chief, his name became something simply inherited
from his father, whom Ikkemotubbe had sold into slavery along
with the Negro grandmother. But as it lost its original significance,
Sam's name came to suggest his role as father to young hunters, an
embodiment in an alien world of the almost forgotten ways of the
Indian inhabitants of the great wilderness.

In addition to the characters taken from earlier stories, "The
Old People" includes a minor figure, the Negro Jimbo. Later he
became Tennie's Jim, Lucas's old brother, James Beauchamp, a
ubiquitous character whose role in the McCaslin stories, though
understated, is important and, to discerning readers, deeply moving.

Besides assembling many of its cast of characters, "The Old
People" anticipated "The Bear" in other ways. Faulkner's earlier
hunting stories had taken place among the trees and the tangles of
brier and cane of the Tallahatchie Bottom, but in this story the
wilderness is personified, becoming at times a living, almost super-

natural thing, no longer simply a background for the hunt. Later Faulkner would stress its vulnerability, but here his emphasis is entirely upon the mystery and power of the great forest, and his language describing it, "tremendous, attentive, impartial, and omniscient," anticipates the grave, almost ponderous style of certain important parts of "The Bear." The nearly impenetrable wilderness is an earthly paradise, which the young narrator enters under the tutelage of Sam who, lost in the modern era, alone knows the way back to the virginal world of the old fathers. At first the immense woods seem alien to men, but they are not. They constitute a friendly and indestructible world in which a boy is allowed to prove himself by killing, and then permitted to find everything more hospitable because death has no ultimate reality. It seemed to him in his youthfulness that when he shot, he saw the slain deer spring "forever immortal" "out of his moment of mortality." Later the boy perceived another buck, "tremendous, unhurried," walking it appeared "out of the very sound of the horn which signified a kill." Sam Fathers's salutation, "Oleh, Chief . . . Grandfather" identifies this apparition as kin to the spirits of his vanished ancestors, the old people themselves. As Quentin's father explains to his son at the end of the story, the dead linger on in places about the earth which they enjoyed while alive. This ghostly buck is an antecedent of Old Ben, the great bear. But in "The Bear" hunting is not an innocent pleasure. In that story killing brings an end to the morally simple world of childhood, whereas in "The Old People" the visionary buck represents a recovery, through killing, of an earthly paradise which had been lost by modern industrialized men.

The two stories that Faulkner wrote in the summer of 1940 but did not publish until later both concerned Negroes. Slavery in the old South is presented nostalgically in "Was," set in 1859, on the eve of the war. "Go Down, Moses," which came out in *Colliers* on January 25, 1941, occurs during the taking of the 1940 census. It deals with the efforts of old Miss Worsham to help Molly Beauchamp bury her grandson, who had been executed in Illinois for murder.

The writing of this story marks a significant stage in the conception of the whole sequence of *Go Down, Moses*. It seems to have originated in Faulkner's seeing a Negro's casket lifted from a train in the Oxford station. At first Faulkner thought of connecting the characters with those of *Absalom, Absalom!*, a novel shaped by a compassionate awareness of the realities of racial relations in the South. In a crossed-out portion of a typescript in the Alderman Library of the University of Virginia, the murderer is named Henry Coldfield Sutpen and his grandmother, Rosa Sutpen. A page discarded during the composition of the story, given by Faulkner to Dan Brennan in July, 1940, concerns Ellen Sutpen, midwife and nurse to most of Jefferson. Probably Ellen was a still earlier name for the grandmother; her nursing and midwifery resemble Molly's role in Zack Edmonds's household (which was described in passages added to the Lucas stories before they were incorporated into *Go Down, Moses*).[4]

Another well-known Yoknapatawpha name which appears in a typescript is Benbow, the original name of Molly's brother Hamp. But while he was still working on the typescript, Faulkner changed all these names. Perhaps he sensed that in its general tone this story was more akin to the stories of other Negroes he had written earlier in the year than to a novel as powerful as *Absalom, Absalom!* His next thought was to rename the Negro murderer Carothers Edmonds Beauchamp, connecting him with both the willful old tenant and his white landlord, who is mentioned in the published story as having driven the youth off his land to Jefferson and a life of crime. The name Carothers Edmonds Beauchamp suggests possible racial mixing in the Edmonds and Beauchamp families, something never suggested in the early versions of the Lucas stories and contrary to the almost comic lightness in treating racial relations characteristic of "Go Down, Moses." The joining in an individual's name of the names of whites as well as blacks meant nothing in itself in southern society. Former slaves like Callie Barr often took their names from the families that had owned them.[5] But this association of names foreshadowed the ultimate development in the published book of the intricately interconnected McCaslin-Beauchamp-Edmonds family. In writing this story Faulkner temporarily abandoned any idea of family entanglements and changed the murderer's name to Samuel Worsham Beauchamp to strengthen the association between Molly and Miss Worsham. But the passing suggestion of a close relationship between the Beauchamps and the Edmonds family was probably the germ of the complex lineal relationships of the completed book. Apart from this suggestion, the principal contributions of this story to the whole were its title and the theme of bondage in the land of Pharaoh which it embodies.

Although "Was" did not appear in print until the book was published, it was written at the same time as the story, "Go Down, Moses," and was originally entitled "Almost."[6] In the early form preserved in a typescript at the University of Virginia, it was told by another of Faulkner's boy narrators, the nine-year-old Bayard Sartoris. While the theme, if not the tone, of "Go Down, Moses" suggested the concerns of *Absalom, Absalom!* and *Light in August*, both the narration and the general handling of "Was" are akin to the humorously affectionate view of the slaveholding South taken in the earlier chapters of *The Unvanquished*. None of the subsequent changes in the story greatly affected its tone. It remains a lighthearted prelude suggesting unpleasant realities only in momentary rufflings of its charming surface. The reader shares almost entirely the nine-year-old Bayard's affection for prewar plantation owners and his unquestioning acceptance of their peculiar social institutions.

In plot, the original version is very close to the later published one. Faulkner's principal changes were in the names of the characters, to relate them to the genealogy of the McCaslin, Edmonds, and Beauchamp families. Bayard arrived with Uncle Buck McCaslin at Primrose, the plantation of Mr. Jason Prim (later renamed Hubert Beauchamp), following a wild horseback chase after a Negro, Tomey's Turl, who was amorously interested in Tennie, one of the Prim slaves. They were received by Mr. Jason and by his sister Sophonsiba (ultimately to become Isaac McCaslin's mother). Bayard stood fascinated before Miss Sophonsiba because "she was the only lady or man either I had ever seen with a roan-colored tooth, and one time Granny and Father was talking about Uncle Buck and Uncle Buddy and Granny said how Miss Sophonsiba had matured into a fine looking woman once." Then Bayard remarked, "I don't know I aint but nine." That night, after several hours of uproarious and futile pursuit of the elusive Turl, Uncle Buck blundered into the occupied bed of husband-hungry Miss Sophonsiba and seemed trapped into marriage. But Bayard fetched to the rescue Buck's twin brother, Uncle Buddy, the somewhat effeminate family cook but a terror with a pack of cards. Mr. Jason had already beaten Buck at drawer poker when Buck had set freedom from Miss Sophonsiba against five hundred dollars he had won from Jason in a bet. But Jason was tempted into another game, this time stud against Buddy, and Buck was liberated, "possible Strait against three Treys in sigt Not called." Jason didn't dare call Buddy. He felt certain that Turl, who dealt, had stacked the deck because it had been agreed that if Buddy won, Turl would be sold to the Prims to marry Tennie.[7]

Not until "Delta Autumn" was written did Isaac McCaslin come into the foreground of a Faulkner story. His role in that story was anticipated by the prominence of the McCaslin twins in "Was." Both Isaac and the twins had had bit parts in stories and novels of the middle and late thirties. Isaac's appearance in "A Bear Hunt" has already been noted. He also had a subordinate part in "Lion" and was mentioned briefly as a storekeeper in "Fool about a Horse," later reworked for *The Hamlet*, and as a farm owner in *The Hamlet* itself. Uncle Buck materialized first in "Retreat," a story revised to become the second chapter of *The Unvanquished*, in which he stopped Bayard and Ringo in the Jefferson square during the Civil War and began raucously shouting his approval of the conduct of Bayard's father, Colonel John Sartoris. In *Absalom, Absalom!* he arrived at Sutpen's Hundred for the burial of Charles Bon, announced that he could pray for any Confederate soldier, and screamed cheers for Sartoris and Forrest. By this time he had acquired the name Theophilus, apparently from the name of the youthful grandson of Uncle Ike mentioned in "Lion." Buck McCaslin had minor roles in two others of the series of stories included in *The Unvanquished*, "Riposte in Tertio" (originally entitled "The Unvanquished") and "Vendée."

The most important step in the development of Faulkner's conception of the McCaslin family before the second version of "The Bear" came with his revision of "Retreat" for publication in *The Unvanquished*, probably late in 1937. Theophilus was given a twin brother Amodeus (Buddy), who won the right to be the family representative in the war and serve as a sergeant in Tennant's brigade in Virginia when past seventy by beating his brother at poker. In this strange interpolation, which has little relation to any-

thing else in *The Unvanquished,* Faulkner gives an extended account of the twins' social theories. These theories, which anticipate
those advocated by the young Isaac McCaslin in the fourth section
of "The Bear," are unexpected from such a crude and shrill sup-
porter of the Confederacy as Buck had seemed until then. According
to the account in *The Unvanquished,* the twin brothers had moved
out of the big "colonial" house their father had built on an extensive
bottomland plantation about fifteen miles from town and were
living in a small log house with "about a dozen dogs." Every night
their Negroes were ceremonially locked in at the front door of the
manor house but allowed to escape all but simultaneously from the
rear to roam the countryside till morning. The McCaslins "believed
that land did not belong to people but that people belonged to land
and that the earth would permit them to live on and out of it and
use it only so long as they behaved and that if they did not behave
right, it would shake them off just like a dog getting rid of fleas."
They devised a complicated plan for having the slaves earn their
freedom by working on the plantation, and they devised a system
for communal use of land with the neighboring dirt farmers, a
system that provided the children with shoes and even a little
schooling.

The McCaslin twins had been evolving in Faulkner's mind for
several years. In "Was" they become fixed with individual distinctiveness. Buck is a notably active, even reckless sixty-year-old,
and Buddy has become sedentary and is now the cook and house-
keeper of the family. He retains his skill at poker, but it seems
unlikely that he could ever have become a sergeant in the Confederate Army. It is not surprising that in later stories Buck becomes
the soldier of the family. Most of the other characters in "Was" were
new, and many were to undergo changes of name or of character
before they reached their final definition in *Go Down, Moses.*

"Delta Autumn," written under the shadow of World War II
late in 1940 or early in 1941, was not published until 1942 when it
appeared in the May-June issue of *Story,* at about the time Random
House brought out *Go Down, Moses.* The magazine version differs
considerably from the later one in the book, and it marks an important stage in the conception of the whole McCaslin saga. For
the first time a hunting story is told in Faulkner's own voice, with-

out the intervention of a fictional narrator. Isaac McCaslin now becomes the center of interest. He is still the aging Uncle Ike of the earlier stories, but the time of the action has been moved up to 1940, and he has been given a distant past to recall. In writing "Delta Autumn," before he got around to revising "The Old People," Faulkner transferred to Isaac McCaslin's boyhood the killing of the buck and the initiation with blood which had been associated in the earlier story with Quentin Compson. These are remembered by Uncle Ike McCaslin as the epochal events of his vanished boyhood. This creation of a youthful past for Isaac McCaslin also serves to associate him for the first time with his spiritual parent, Sam Fathers.

The Isaac McCaslin of *Go Down, Moses*—developed from the old hunter of "Delta Autumn," the youthful ones of "The Old People," and the early version of "The Bear" published in the *Saturday Evening Post*, and also resembling the Bayard Sartoris of *The Unvanquished*—is an ordinary, decent, sane, moderately intelligent human being. He is therefore almost unique among the protagonists of Faulkner's major novels. Consider the principal portraits in the gallery: the Compsons—Benjy, Quentin, Jason, and Caddy; the Bundrens—Darl, Cash, Jewell, Vardaman, and Anse; Horace Benbow, Temple Drake, and Popeye; Gail Hightower, Joanna Burden, and Joe Christmas; the Quentin Compson of *Absalom, Absalom!* and Thomas Sutpen; Ike, Mink and Flem Snopes. Faulkner was obsessed with moral issues from first to last, but until almost all his greatest work was completed, his imagination was fired almost exclusively by characters incapable of normal human life. With the important exception of Addie Bundren,[8] the characters whose inner lives are presented with great imaginative sympathy are idiots, criminals, neurotics, and madmen—the ghost-obsessed, the sexually warped, the morally stunted, and those incapable of effective action. With the creation of Isaac McCaslin, Faulkner moves toward the central moral tradition of the realistic novel. Later Faulkner's shift toward realism in *The Town*, after the imaginative extravagance of *The Hamlet*, led to dullness and failure. But in *Go Down, Moses* realism in characterization creates a moral intensity unique in Faulkner's work.

"The Old People," though set in November, was a young man's story. "Delta Autumn" is thoroughly autumnal. It seems to reflect something of the national disillusionment of the years about 1940, darkened as it is by references to lingering economic depression, domestic fascism, and threatening war in Europe. Uncle Ike, the last of the old hunters, journeys once again back to the shrunken tangle of wilderness, now two hundred miles from Jefferson, to spend two weeks with the sons and grandsons of his former companions. At one time he had a wife and children, "though no more,"[9] and he lives only for the weeks spent under canvas each November. He is old, hunters are not what they once were, and the great woods themselves are nearing extinction.

At times old Isaac believes that the wilderness is not being destroyed but is simply retreating voluntarily after having served its purpose. For a moment he is able to conceive of himself and the wilderness as contemporaries dwindling away together, "not into oblivion, nothingness, but into a scope free of both time and space" like the world of the old people where the immortal game would run "forever before the tireless belling immortal hounds, falling and rising phoenix-like before the soundless guns." But more characteristic of this story is McCaslin's tired pessimism, pervaded by nostalgia for a heroic past and mourning for the lost woods ravished by human selfishness. He has renounced ownership of land because he believes that the land should belong to no one person but to all. Men in their petty greed have refused to use it properly.

The woods of "The Old People" had been an earthly paradise capable of fulfilling all the aspirations of a maturing boy. The returning hunters of "Delta Autumn" bring outside troubles back with them into the diminishing sanctuary. As the story opens, the landscape itself seems to be dissolving away under the November rain, and the conversation of the hunters is soured by memories of the depression and thoughts of Hitler and of approaching war. Against the cynicism of his younger companion, Don Boyd,[10] old Isaac speaks with the simple patriotism of an earlier generation. But before the end of the story he is placed in a situation which makes his moral affirmations seem futile and pathetic. A girl with whom Boyd has been having an affair arrives in his tent carrying an infant. While trying to force upon her money left behind by Boyd, Isaac discovers that she is a Negro. Taken aback, he is able only to wail, "Cant nobody do nothing for you," and he advises her to forget about Boyd, to go North and "find a black man who would see in you what it was you saw in him, who would ask nothing of you and expect less and get even still less if it's revenge you want." She looks quietly at McCaslin and then asks, "Old man . . . have you lived so long that you have forgotten all you ever knew or felt or even heard about love?"

With this confrontation in the tent, Faulkner for the first time brings racial injustice into the great wilderness. His associating the destruction of the woods with Boyd's indifference to the girl and to his child anticipates his associating in "The Bear" the death of Old Ben and a boy's discovering the evil in his family's past. But there is an odd inconsistency in Isaac McCaslin's attitude in "Delta Autumn," an inconsistency which Faulkner himself seems to have shared to some extent. McCaslin is shocked by Boyd's behavior toward the girl, but he also believes that the relationship with her was inherently bad. His initial thought is that it will be a millennium or two before love between a white man and a black girl will be possible in America. But later his view becomes more negative. He concludes his great lament for the despoiled Delta, which develops directly out of his recognition of Don Boyd's inhumanity, with a nightmare account of *"Chinese and African and Aryan and Jew"* who *"all breed and spawn together until no man has time to say which is which."* Love which violates racial boundaries in itself, as well as the behavior of a Boyd, is something that will accomplish the revenge of the desecrated land. Despite Faulkner's extensive revision of "Delta Autumn" to prepare it for *Go Down, Moses,* a revision which tied it more closely to the intricate and unhappy history of the McCaslin family and which subtly altered the portrayal of Isaac, the reference to interracial—and interreligious—spawning remained unaltered.

CHAPTER THREE

THE FIRST VERSION OF "THE BEAR"

A STORY ENTITLED "The Bear" was published in the May 11, 1942, issue of the *Saturday Evening Post*. It had been written a year or so earlier, in all likelihood shortly after Faulkner had finished the magazine version of "Delta Autumn." He had kept it out of print, as he had "Delta Autumn," until *Go Down, Moses* was ready for publication. Evidently he wished to publish this first version of "The Bear" but did not wish it to be seen until the later, more complex version contained in the book was in print. The earlier "Bear" concerns an unnamed boy not yet identified as Isaac McCaslin but described in such a way that he could not be Quentin Compson, the boy protagonist of "Lion" and the earlier versions of "The Old People." Strangely, Faulkner seems not to have seen young Isaac immediately as the central figure of "The Bear" even though he had associated his boyhood with Sam Fathers in writing "Delta Autumn." But he does include a passing reference to the killing of the buck and the marking with blood, and he makes certain modifications of detail which suggest that his imagination was groping its way closer to the final form of the McCaslin family saga. The young

Negro who appeared in "The Old People" as Jimbo, and who ultimately became Lucas's brother James, is here named Tennie's Jim.
Faulkner already had come to think of him as the son of Tennie,
the girl whom the McCaslin slave, Turl, ran away to visit in "Was."
There is, however, at this point no suggestion that Jim has any
white blood. He is referred to as "the Negro," and Sam Fathers,
who has been made the son rather than the grandson of the
Chickasaw chief, is mentioned as "the Indian." More is made of
Sam's mixed blood than in "The Old People," but real emphasis on
his being part Negro came only in the final version of the story. General Compson joins the hunters for the first time, in a sense taking
the place of the elderly Uncle Ike McCaslin who had been the
senior member of the hunting party in the earlier stories. The hunts
on the Tallahatchie bottom had, as one story followed another, been
gradually shifted farther back in time. Faulkner's addition of General Compson would seem to place the action of the first version of
"The Bear" before 1900, the year of the general's death according to
the Compson chronology Faulkner later appended to *The Sound
and the Fury*.

The original version of "The Bear" is to some degree a rewriting
of "The Old People." Once again a white boy is brought into com-
munion with the wilderness by Sam Fathers, has an encounter with
a mysterious animal to mark his initiation and mastery, and, finally,
discusses the experience with his father. Another source is "Lion,"
which concerned a great dog's pursuit of Old Ben, "an extra bear—
the head bear." In his reminiscences of *Old Times in the Faulkner
Country*, John Cullen relates Old Ben to an actual animal, Old
Reelfoot, who had lost two toes on the left front paw and left tracks
eight inches wide. Bear hunting had entered Faulkner's fiction as
early as *Sartoris* (1929), in which young Bayard found among his
brother John's mementos the withered paw of his first bear, killed
in the bottom when he was twelve. Perhaps T. B. Thorpe's nine-
teenth-century story of "The Big Bear of Arkansas," a "creation
bar" who was unhuntable but who came in and died when his time
had come, had some influence on Faulkner's evolving conception of
Old Ben. In "Lion" the bear had been notable enough to merit a
human name rather than "Two Toe" or some such typical bear

name, but the animal which was most celebrated was the huge, topaz-eyed hunting dog for whom the story was named. In the earlier version of "The Bear," Lion is replaced by another dog, a fyce which is his equal in bravery but which exists on a lower level of being than Old Ben. The bear is no longer simply an extraordinarily formidable animal; he has become a mythic figure looming in the boy's dreams out of "the limbo from which time emerged." He is a leftover out of the past, an "apotheosis of the old wild life" which is about to be destroyed. "Indomitable and alone," he is likened to "Old Priam reft of his old wife and having outlived all his sons."[1]

In writing "The Bear," Faulkner drew on his three earlier hunting stories. The bear first appeared in "Lion," but he resembles the mysterious buck addressed as "Grandfather" in "The Old People." That buck was an immortal spirit which had seemed to walk out of the sound of the horn signifying its death. Here the bear is revered as an invincible creature in celebration of whose "furious immortality" a yearly hunt is made. But the wilderness the hunters visit in their annual pilgrimage is no longer the invulnerable immensity of "The Old People." Some foreboding of "Delta Autumn" already hangs over it; its edges are under constant though trivial attack by ax and plow. And the bear shares in the vulnerability of the woods. Although he is a supernatural being "absolved of mortality," he is also a "mortal animal" who can be killed if a really formidable hunting dog can be found. In "The Old People" Faulkner had presented two bucks, one which was killed by the boy hunter and another which would exist forever. In "The Bear" both bucks are united in the one bear.

One difference between "The Bear" and "The Old People" is in Faulkner's increased concern with the moral values involved in hunting. For a boy to stand in wait for a deer required no great courage, and to kill brought no anguish. Sam Fathers could easily assure Mr. Compson that his son had "done all right." Shooting the physical buck in the morning brought about the appearance of the metaphysical one in the afternoon. But stalking a bear is a dangerous enterprise, and death is treated with such gravity in "The Bear" that hunting possesses a poignancy it lacked in the earlier story. After years of trailing the bear, learning to find his print, the boy comes to realize that he is vulnerable if a powerful enough dog can be found. With this realization comes, pretty much coincidentally, a growing awareness of the boy's own mortality and of his need to master his fear, to be, as Sam says, "scared" but not "afraid" if he is to be worthy of the bear who willingly exposes himself to the hunters' guns in order to savor his freedom. Finally, after he has accepted a condition in which the usual relationship between the hunter and the hunted has been abolished by his relinquishing his gun and giving up the "three lifeless mechanicals," the watch, the compass, and the stick, the boy is granted his visionary experience of the bear.

Some years after this climactic moment, in the earlier version of "The Bear," the boy's father tries to help him to understand why on another occasion when he had an opportunity to kill the bear he did not shoot but, instead, rushed under him to rescue his foolhardy little dog.[2] In the office of the plantation, a room consecrated by the talk of brave men and by the animals "ordered and compelled by and within the wilderness . . . by the ancient and immitigable rules which voided all regrets and brooked no quarter," the father reads Keats's "Ode on a Grecian Urn," stressing the final lines of the second stanza: "She cannot fade, though thou hast not thy bliss/for ever wilt thou love, and she be fair." The boy, like the rest of us, has some difficulty understanding exactly what his father has in mind when he says that Keats was talking about truth, about "courage and honor and pride, and pity and love of justice and of liberty. They all touch the heart, and what the heart holds to becomes truth, as far as we know truth." The boy recalls the whole experience: the old bear who willingly risked his own life; Sam, the "son of a Negro slave and an Indian king . . . who had learned humility through suffering, and pride through . . . endurance"; and the dog, who was too small to be proud or dangerous, or even humble, and therefore could only be brave. He finally senses that the virtues of the heart include compassion as well as bravery and endurance. In his refusing to kill the animal he loved, he has shown the humility needed to balance his pride, which was involved in mastering the woods. Having achieved through renunciation a moral strength comparable to that of Old Ben, Sam, and the small dog, he possesses truth which is timeless. His achievement, like the love of the youth on the Grecian urn, will never perish because his action was never consummated. Later Faulkner's feelings about Isaac McCaslin's renunciation became ambivalent; the whole discussion of abstaining from shooting is recalled in the later version of "The Bear" in a context which makes judging the moral value of any kind of action very difficult. But there can be no doubt that he originally regarded the boy's renunciation of the kill with admiration.

In writing the first "Bear," Faulkner came to realize that the narrative method of "The Old People" had been a mistake; he decided to follow "Delta Autumn" and relate the story in his own voice. He never found the device of the child narrator really congenial, never used it with the skill and delicacy of Mark Twain or Sherwood Anderson. In using fictional narrators of any age, he was willing to mute his own voice only to a limited extent. The voices of the different narrators of *Absalom, Absalom!* are distinguishable, but they lack the distinctiveness of a Huckleberry Finn or a Holden Caulfield. Faulkner characteristically immerses his reader in the experience being described. Undue emphasis upon the individuality of his narrator would distract readers from the intensity of the experience itself. Usually, the voices of Faulkner's narrators blend with his own voice. At the end of *Absalom, Absalom!* when Quentin Compson desperately thinks of the South—"I dont hate it . . . I dont. I dont! I dont hate it! I dont hate it!"—his thoughts cannot entirely be distinguished from Faulkner's, or, for that matter, from the reader's.

In "Lion" and in the early versions of "Was" and "The Old People," Faulkner had conveyed the story in the words of youthful narrators. But he made so little effort to adapt his material to the youthful consciousness of the narrators that the latter two stories could be converted to Faulkner's own narration without significant alteration of substance. "Was," which depends upon the naïveté of a child's sense of people, actions, and events, might seem more effectively told by the child; but it is even better shifted into Faulkner's voice, which is limited for the most part to the child's point of view. Even the passage describing the appearance of Miss Sophonsiba is enhanced as we watch the boy standing "quietly a little behind Uncle Buck, watching her lips until they opened and he could see the roan tooth." A moment later she said something about a bumblebee, and Faulkner tells us that

he couldn't remember that. It was too fast and there was too much of it, the earrings and beads clashing and jingling like little trace chains on a toy mule trotting and the perfume stronger too, like the earrings and beads sprayed it out each time they moved and he watched the roan-colored tooth flick and glint between her lips; something about Uncle Buck was a bee sipping from flower to flower and not staying long anywhere and all that stored sweetness to be wasted on Uncle Buddy's desert air.

Faulkner uses his own voice to suggest both what attracted the boy's attention and the implications he missed which the reader should not.

Little that Faulkner wished to convey in "The Old People" came naturally from a child narrator. The rich, often latinate, language seemed implausible for a boy to use. Reference to the first buck "looking not like a ghost but as if all of light were condensed in him and he were the source of it"; to the wilderness, "tremendous, attentive, impartial, and omniscient"; and to the "eye of the ancient immortal Umpire" all seemed more suitable when Faulkner later transposed them to his own voice.

Liberated from any effort at narration through a child, the style of the earlier version of "The Bear" reflects Faulkner's increasingly complex feelings about the hunt and the wilderness. The opening paragraphs, though less opaque than certain passages in the first and fourth sections of the expanded version of the story, have something of the denseness of the great wilderness itself. The first sentence, "He was ten," offers no difficulty, but the second, "But it had already begun," forces the reader to grope for the meaning of "it." At first "it" seems to refer specifically to the bear, but it comes to incorporate not only the wilderness and the hunt but, finally, the meaning of the entire experience. The opening paragraphs are not limited to the boy's point of view. References range far beyond his youthful understanding as the reader is told of the doomed wilderness being destroyed by the pettiness of man and of the old bear who had won a name in a land where men were nameless to each other. The conception of the bear as "an anachronism, indomitable and invincible, out of the old dead time, a phantom, epitome and apotheosis" of the life of the wilderness is one scarcely likely to occur to a preadolescent boy. Yet the general effect of these paragraphs is to relate the reader's feelings to the boy's; perhaps the feelings are those the boy will have when he grows old enough to understand fully what he has been involved in. For all his freedom of reference, Faulkner confines us to the boy's thoughts, dreams, and actions. At moments of particular tension, we are the boy as he stood "for a moment, alien and small in the green and topless solitude" or as, looking up as the wilderness solidified, he "saw the bear. It did not emerge, appear; it was just there immobile, solid, fixed in the hot dappling of the green and windless noon, not as big as he had dreamed it, but as big as he had expected it, bigger, dimensionless, against the dappled obscurity."

The earlier version of "The Bear," which culminates in the dreamlike vision of Old Ben, immobile in the green and dappled forest of a windless noon, is, like "The Old People," a simple tale of a boy's moral education, and it is an unambiguous celebration of the negative virtue of abnegation. Yet hints, scarcely developed within this version, of the bear's mortal vulnerability contain the germs of the greater moral complexity and greater moral truth of the ultimate account of the story.

PART TWO

"The Bear"

CHAPTER FOUR

SECTIONS ONE TO THREE

STORY BY STORY, as he wrote his way from "Lion" on through the first version of "The Bear," Faulkner's conception of the hunt gradually developed, taking on more and more complex significance. But the accomplishment of the final form of "The Bear" was a work of synthesis immensely greater than anything which had preceded it. Sections one through three and section five weld together "Lion," a story of the hunt which ended in the deaths of the huge dog and Old Ben, and the earlier version of "The Bear," an account of a boy's attainment of virtue demonstrated by his abstaining from killing. Section four brings in the tangled history of the McCaslin family and of the South, relating a recognition of the evil of slavery to the death of the bear.

The cast of characters includes many familiar figures and some fresh creations. Young Isaac McCaslin has at last assumed his place as protagonist, and the opening paragraph picks out for special attention two other men and two animals: Boon Hogganbeck, the part Indian who kills the bear; Sam Fathers; Old Ben; and the mongrel, Lion. Only the last three, Faulkner writes, "were taintless

and incorruptible." In addition to these, the most important par-
ticipants in the hunt are Major de Spain, old General Compson, the
ubiquitous Tennie's Jim, and a new character, Isaac's cousin
(Carothers)[1] McCaslin Edmonds, who took over the role played by
the boy's father in the earlier version of "The Bear" and who was to
replace Mr. Compson when "The Old People" was rewritten.

The McCaslin family history, like the events of the great hunt
for Old Ben, had been germinating in Faulkner's mind since the
middle thirties. The final pattern of McCaslin genealogy[2] is revealed
when in the fourth section Isaac examines the ledgers kept by his
father, Uncle Buck, and his father's twin brother, Uncle Buddy. He
then learns of his grandfather and of his black relatives who are
called Beauchamp. Isaac himself first appeared in 1934 in a minor
role as an old man in "A Bear Hunt," and his father, Uncle Buck,
materialized in the same year in "Retreat." The characters of the
twin brothers of the Civil War generation, Theophilus and Amodeus,
had reached nearly final definition in the revision for book publication of the stories of *The Unvanquished*. Yet neither there nor in
the original version of "Was" was there any suggestion of white
blood in the McCaslin slaves. There were striking anticipations of
the McCaslin chronicle in *Absalom, Absalom!* Thomas Sutpen, the
ruthless, driven embodiment of the old South, who tore a plantation
out of a hundred square miles of junglelike bottomland and dis-
owned his son when he discovered the boy was tainted with Negro
blood, resembles the original McCaslin, old Carothers, who, as
Isaac sensed, could not lower himself to say "my son to a nigger."
The path of Thomas Sutpen's life from frontier cabin to the great
house of Sutpen's Hundred was traveled in the opposite direction
by Isaac McCaslin in his renunciation of his landed heritage for an
ancestral musket. An especially striking indication of the way
Absalom, Absalom! contained things Faulkner would develop in
Go Down, Moses is the anticipation of the behavior of Carothers
McCaslin in General Compson's supposing for a time (in the earlier
book) that the younger Bon was the son of Sutpen's black daughter,
Clytie, "got by its father on the body of his own daughter."

Recall, also, that in writing the story "Go Down, Moses" in the
summer of 1940, Faulkner first thought of connecting the black
murderer with the families of *Absalom, Absalom!* Next he had tried

the name Carothers Edmonds Beauchamp, which recalled the white
landowner of "A Point of Law" and "Gold Is Not Always." But
ultimately it was not to what in the end became the Edmonds
branch of the McCaslin family that he related Lucas Beauchamp.
No story published before the fourth part of the later version of
"The Bear" suggests that Lucas carries any white blood, but there
is a genealogical chart in the Alderman Library which marks an
earlier stage of Faulkner's effort to tie together in "The Bear" the
various stories of *Go Down, Moses* by making Lucas a relative of
Isaac McCaslin and connecting the Edmonds and McCaslin families
by marriage.

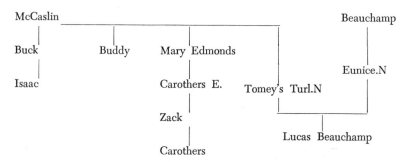

The genealogy of both the main white and the Edmonds branch of
the McCaslin family is substantially the same as the version published in part four of "The Bear."[3] The Edmonds line moves from
the contemporary Carothers back to his father, Zack, who had been
mentioned in "Gold Is Not Always." Then it goes to the earlier
Carothers, usually referred to in *Go Down, Moses* as McCaslin or
Cass Edmonds, and to Mary Edmonds, the sister of Buck and
Buddy, who is never mentioned by name except in this chart. In
the McCaslin line Isaac no longer has the children mentioned in
the magazine version of "Delta Autumn," and the progenitor has
been given no Christian name; he is simply McCaslin. Eventually,
he was called Lucius Quintus Carothers, a resounding name which
associates him with Carothers Edmonds and Lucas Beauchamp.
Faulkner later suggested that Lucas had simply altered his name a
trifle from Lucius to Lucas Quintus Carothers McCaslin Beauchamp
to make it uniquely his own. The name L. Q. C. McCaslin also
recalls that of Oxford's greatest man, the former Confederate officer

who became a senator, secretary of the interior under Cleveland, justice of the Supreme Court, and the subject of one of John Kennedy's *Profiles in Courage*, Lucius Quintus Cincinnatus Lamar.

The other lines of descent in the chart are farther from the final order, though Faulkner has moved beyond the first version of "Was" in making Turl a blood member of the McCaslin family. Neither Tomey nor Tennie—Turl's mother and wife—is listed, but their existence is implied by the chart. The Beauchamp lineage is sketchy. No white members are specifically named, and there is no suggestion of marital connection with the McCaslins. It is clear from this chart that Faulkner had already considered giving Lucas's name to a white family but had not yet thought of attaching it to the owners of Tennie. Contrary to his final scheme, Faulkner has put Negro blood into both the McCaslin and Beauchamp family lines. Eunice, whom he later made the grandmother of Turl, is placed on the Beauchamp side, and Lucas descends from blacks in both families, not just from McCaslin ones. No mention is made of Tennie's Jim, Turl's son, who in the end was to become Lucas's brother, James Thucydides Beauchamp.

Faulkner began the second version of "The Bear" with an allusion to the first: "There was a man and a dog too this time." "This time," in 1883, the boy is sixteen, the age of Quentin in "Lion," although Faulkner almost immediately shifts back to his earlier years of waiting and then of learning to become a hunter, which he had described in the first "Bear." In place of the fyce that had taught him, at fourteen, humility and pride through its courage, the principal dog is Lion, the great beast of the early hunting story, who loves nothing and has the impersonal malignance of a destructive natural force. The man is again Sam Fathers, the boy's mentor and now also the trainer of Lion. Despite the shift in the story's balance suggested by this association of Sam, the boy's moral tutor, with the fated antagonist of the bear he loved, the opening section is not substantially different from the original version. There are changes, rhetorical embellishments of the softly focused long views of the immense wilderness and of the mythical bear, amplifications of detail in the carefully engraved closeups. The almost ceremonial seriousness of the opening has been heightened by shifting forward to the second paragraph the description of the hunters reverently talking of and drinking to the men and dogs, deer, and bear who played heroic and ordered roles in the chase. This passage had originally been placed just before the reading of the "Ode on a Grecian Urn" and the discussion of the boy's abstaining from shooting the bear. In addition, Faulkner inserted an extended description of young Isaac's first trip to the wilderness, through a slow drizzle barely above the freezing point, during which he watched "the tall and endless wall of dense November woods under the dissolving afternoon and the year's death, sombre, impenetrable," which he would enter to meet the waiting Sam Fathers. Of the passages taken over from the first version, the most carefully rewritten was the concluding one telling of Ike's early-morning hunt through wet gray woods, which culminated in the bear's revealing himself in the sun-dappled noontime, after the boy had relinquished his human advantages and had become lost in a wilderness growing more and more strange. In the morning as the boy moves alone through the woods, at first swiftly and then more deliberately, exhibiting the skill acquired from years of Sam's tutelage, Faulkner gives the reader a fuller account than he gave in the earlier version of the boy's thoughts and sensations; but once the bear is present, he concentrates entirely upon rendering its visionary appearance. One significant change is the amplified account of the bear's footprints. Originally Faulkner had mentioned a single crooked print which the boy watched fill with water. The altered description is used to suggest the boy's loss of bearings in a world become suddenly fluid. He watches the water begin to overflow the print and make its sides dissolve away and then sees another and then still others forming mysteriously before him "as though they were being shaped out of thin air just one constant pace short of where he would lose them forever and be lost forever himself." Then suddenly the wilderness solidified, and Old Ben "was just there."

The second section is a bridge between the material derived from the first version of "The Bear" and that derived from "Lion," which forms the basis of parts three and five. It includes the fyce episode of the earlier version and new material concerning the capture and training of the huge dog, Lion, (whose name had been used as the title of the whole story until just before *Go Down, Moses* was sent to the printer). In this section the bear seems to be of the natural order, a formidable but vulnerable animal, as he had been in "Lion," the earliest of the stories of the hunt. The discussion of the boy's not shooting the fyce, which had concluded the earlier version of "The Bear," is omitted and kept for use in the fourth section. Instead, Ike and Sam are portrayed considering the mortality of the bear, realizing that someone will get him sometime. The boy wishes that it be either one of them "so it wont be until the last day. When even he dont want it to last any longer." Then Faulkner inserts the conditional statement he had first used as the section's opening sentence and would use once again at the beginning of the concluding paragraph: "So he should have hated and feared Lion."

In the original story Lion had been a magnificent creature for whose favor Boon Hogganbeck and the Negro cook, Ad (later renamed Ash), had competed. His death had marked the end of the heroic age of the woods. Now it is Old Ben's life on which the continuance of the old wild life of the natural world is dependent. Yet Isaac McCaslin and Sam Fathers, the hunters who most partake of that life, do not hate and fear Lion. They accept him with a sense of inevitability which seems in some respects related to the spirit of "Delta Autumn." Sam captures and trains Lion, turning him over to Boon only when his training has been completed. The old man senses from the beginning what the discovery of Lion forebodes, and Isaac soon comes to understand. Faulkner writes that years later, when Isaac had become a man, he would fully comprehend that Sam saw in Lion his own death as well as the death of the bear and the destruction of the old wilderness. He would realize that Sam was old and childless and had had for seventy years to be black, that he had been glad to sense that it was almost over. Even at the time Lion was captured, the boy had an intuitive sense of what was involved. Somberly, but with none of the bitterness of the old man of "Delta Autumn," he accepted the coming loss of the three things he most loved—the woods, the bear, and Sam Fathers. The second section concludes with his realization that something had already begun, "the beginning of the end of something, he didn't know what except that he would not grieve. He would be humble and proud that he had been found worthy to be a part of it too or even just to see it too."

In "Lion" the last chase had taken place in the coldest December the boy narrator had known. On a day too cold for hunting Boon had been dispatched with a suitcase to Memphis for whiskey, and the boy had been sent along to see that most, if not all, of the whiskey got back to the camp.[4] An account of their trip, shifted back into the nineteenth century[5] but only slightly modified, opens the third section of "The Bear," which returns to the boy's sixteenth year, the time mentioned at the beginning of the story. The journey in hunting clothes, first by log train and then by passenger train, went pleasantly until they reached the busy pavements of the city. Then Boon looked as if he should never have been let out of the woods or out of reach of some adult who could tell strangers, "Don't be afraid. He wont hurt you." After some difficulty the boy got Boon back on the train, and when they climbed into the caboose of the log train at sundown, he realized that there would be no frost and that on the next day Lion would have the third of his annual races after Old Ben.

In the next portion of the third section, the account of that day's chase, Faulkner made substantial changes. In "Lion" the boy had returned to camp after several futile hours at a hunting stand where he had heard only the distant baying of the dogs. Then came a long uneasy wait, while he looked out into unceasing rain and then darkness, for word of how the pursuit had gone. Suddenly into the room came Boon, claw-slashed and dripping blood, carrying Lion in his coat. The most moving thing in the story was Boon's grief over the mortally wounded dog, his refusal of attention for himself, and his desperate mule ride to Hoke's for a doctor. The details of his killing the bear with a knife are disclosed indirectly, almost as an afterthought, as if only to reveal the heroic dimensions of his love for Lion.

In "The Bear" the day's events are narrated directly and in chronological order. Although the death of the bear carries a significance beyond anything in the earlier story, the tone is not substantially altered. In the second section Faulkner had suggested that Sam Fathers and Isaac had not feared but had almost welcomed Lion as part of the fated order of things, even though they realized that he meant the death of Old Ben. Here Faulkner modified only slightly the sympathetic portrayal of the killers of the bear which he had created in "Lion." The courage and heroism of Boon and Lion are even more impressive. Lion's virtues are limited a little more narrowly to those which contribute to the pursuit and the kill. But Boon is made more innocent. His incompetence with a gun is again stressed; whereas in the earlier story he had, in a sort of duel, shot a black man in the face after missing four times, in "The Bear" he is described as having managed only to smash a plate glass window and hit a passing black woman in the leg.

Faulkner devotes about four pages to Isaac's impressions of the final hectic race after the bear. The curiously quiet, almost anticlimactic death that takes place before the boy's eyes is merely an amplification of the indirect presentation of the action in "Lion." He crashes through the underbrush on his mule, dismounts in time to see Old Ben rise from the ground with Lion's jaws locked to his throat and begin to rake the dog's belly with his foreclaws. Then Boon rushes in, knife in hand, hurdling over hounds, and "for an instant they almost resembled a piece of statuary: the clinging dog, the bear, the man stride its back, working and probing the buried blade." The bear topples over and then surges upright, takes a few steps toward the woods and then crashes. "It didn't collapse, crumble. It fell all of a piece, as a tree falls, so that all three of them, man, dog and bear, seemed to bounce once."

In the more than thirteen pages of section three which follow, Faulkner made little more of the bear's death than he had in "Lion" where his primary concern was with the fatally injured dog. The bear lying dead in the yard, "his lips snarled back from his worn teeth," even with fifty-two lumps under his skin from old bullets, "buckshot, rifle and ball," seems merely a dead bear. Lion seems the more significant animal as he lies dying on the gallery, opening his eyes every so often for a last glimpse of the woods, as a crowd of men gather to talk quietly "of hounds and bear and deer and men of yesterday vanished from the earth."

Sam Fathers had not been a member of the hunting party in "Lion." The only black had been the cook, Ad, Boon's rival for the huge dog's affection. Sam's part in the final hunt in "The Bear" was inconspicuous, but his death, mysteriously related to Old Ben's, was given extraordinary emphasis. Just after the bear's final fall, Sam is discovered by Tennie's Jim face down in the trampled mud. No one is able to explain what has happened. But the boy knew that Sam also was going to die. He understood the look in his eyes which saw beyond "the death of a bear and the dying of a dog." He understood the significance of Sam's saying to Major de Spain when they reached his hut, "Let me out, master. . . . Let me go home."

Ike best comprehends Sam's feelings, but Tennie's Jim and Boon were also in the woods when he died. The other members of the hunting party left when Major de Spain broke camp, after Lion died at sundown on Thursday. General Compson's intervention secured Ike permission to stay on with Sam until Sunday. But on Saturday Jim rode thirty miles to bring back Ike's cousin, McCaslin Edmonds, and Major de Spain. As the sun rose Sunday, they approached a low ridge in the wilderness and discovered beyond the mound of Lion's grave a blanket-covered bundle placed on a platform of saplings suspended between four posts. McCaslin demanded of Boon, "Did you kill him . . . ?" Staggering as if drunk against a tree, and then catching himself and "backing with the tree's trunk his wild spent scoriated face and the tremendous heave and collapse of his chest," Boon denied that he had. Section three concludes with Ike's interrupting to prevent further questioning, shouting at McCaslin, "Leave him alone! . . . Goddamn it! Leave him alone!"

At the conclusion of "The Bear"'s three early sections devoted to hunting, three of the four animals and men mentioned in the opening paragraph are dead, the three who were incorruptible. Only Boon remains. He has killed Old Ben and, apparently, Sam Fathers, perhaps in some ritual like that followed in the mysterious death of the Indian Jobaker, in "The Old People." Boon may be corruptible, as the final tragicomic scene of "The Bear" suggests, but he has killed in innocence. He killed the bear out of love for Lion, and he killed Sam because Sam wanted to die. In his own blundering way he was as powerfully affected by Sam's death as Ike was, and he was much less able to comprehend it. Isaac can accept Sam Fathers's wish to die and therefore he is able to understand that Boon's killings were acts of love. He has matured and is no longer the virginal youth of the first version of "The Bear." The wilderness has given him, at sixteen, an awareness of death and of some of the things that limit all human life.

CHAPTER FIVE

THE FOURTH SECTION

THE FOURTH SECTION, unlike the story's other parts, which had grown
out of things contained in the earlier version of "The Bear" or in
"Lion," was a fresh creation of 1941.[1] Placed out of chronological
order so that it is read before the description in section five of
events which happened three years earlier, section four is as long
and complex as all the other four sections of "The Bear" put together.
After several readings the relations between its varied and confusing parts and the relation between it as a whole and the rest of
"The Bear" become relatively clear. Once this happens, we see that
this section is the genealogical and emotional center of *Go Down,
Moses.*

The importance and the confusing complexity of section four—
concerning the meaning of which there can probably never be entire
agreement—make desirable a very thorough and careful consider-
ation of its elements. The very long, rambling, and interrupted
dispute between Isaac McCaslin and his cousin, the discovery of
the McCaslin family history in the plantation ledgers, the scene of
grotesque lovemaking between Isaac and his wife, and even, per-

haps, the wild tale of Hubert Fitz-Hubert Beauchamp's legacy to his nephew give force and meaning to the stories which precede and follow "The Bear" in *Go Down, Moses*. These stories would be far less substantial if they stood by themselves. In section four is the place of juncture of the stories concerned with the lives and deaths blacks endure in the white South and those dealing with Isaac McCaslin's taking refuge from the South in the great woods that he loved. Previously, Faulkner, save for a passing suggestion of what it meant to Sam Fathers to be black, had brought the theme of racial injustice into the wilderness world only in "Delta Autumn."

When first read, section four seems a wordy chaos from the depths of which a confusing variety of phrases and images are whirled to the surface without regard to chronology, so that they lodge in the mind of the bewildered reader like individual lines and blobs of color spun out from the swirling whole of a canvas of Jackson Pollock. Images: a slave woman wading to her death on Christmas Day, the opening of a gleaming coffeepot stuffed with scraps of I.O.U.'s, a grotesque scene of sexual temptation in a Jefferson boardinghouse, a gaunt rainswept cabin in Arkansas. Phrases: "then he was twenty one . . . and nothing more . . . and he . . . 1888 the man, repudiated denied and free . . . and McCaslin . . . Escape . . . Then he was sixteen . . . all things that touch the heart . . . not to mention 1865 . . . father's Will . . . 1895 and husband but no father . . . I'm free, she said . . . and that was all . . . Dispossessed of Eden."

The settings of this section are on the cleared land, not in the wilderness; primarily, they are the commissary and dining room of the McCaslin plantation and rented rooms in Jefferson. At the conclusion of the previous section, Isaac had proved himself capable of accepting the inevitable deaths of Old Ben and Sam Fathers, and of understanding and accepting Boon's role in those deaths. Section three had concluded with Ike in tears, defending Boon against McCaslin Edmonds's pressing questions, shouting "leave him alone!" Section four opens with the phrase "then he was twenty-one," a phrase which would be repeated as the phrase "so he should have hated and feared Lion" had been repeated in the second section. It alludes to the birthday on which a man officially becomes an adult, on which he is recognized by the state as mature and wise enough to be trusted to vote. Faulkner's reader is led to associate, naturally enough, the phrase "then he was twenty-one" with the wisdom just demonstrated in the defense of Boon and to expect a wiser Isaac McCaslin in the new section. But Faulkner surprises us. He did not regard wisdom as the inevitable result of chronological aging, and Ike reveals himself as less mature in coping with the complexities of life on the cleared land at twenty-one than he had shown himself in the wilderness at sixteen. Now he confronts the complexity of the evil inevitable in human society as he comes into his patrimony and marries. Isaac receives two differing legacies, but his are not the only inheritances considered, nor is his the only marriage. Faulkner also includes accounts of the legacies Isaac's black relatives received in the will of his grandfather, Carothers McCaslin, as well as an account of the marriage of one these relatives.

A Negro lineage different from the one proposed in the genealogical chart in the Alderman Library is disclosed.[2] Lucas Beauchamp has been made the son of Tomey's Turl (Terrel) and Tennie, who were married shortly after the poker game in "Was." Tennie's Jim has become Lucas's brother, and they have been given a sister, Fonsiba (Sophonsiba). Turl's mother, Tomey (Thomasina), is the daughter of Eunice, the wife of Thucydides (Thucydus) who had been brought from Carolina with his parents, Roscius (Roskus) and Phoebe (Fibby), by Isaac McCaslin's grandfather.

Eunice had been related to the Beauchamp family in the genealogical chart in the Alderman Library; in the final scheme of "The Bear" Faulkner made her the mistress of old Carothers McCaslin. He gave Lucas's name, Beauchamp, to the nearby white plantation family who were called Prim in the early version of "Was." Jason was renamed Hubert Fitz-Hubert Beauchamp, but Miss Sophonsiba, who became the mother of Isaac McCaslin, retained her given name. Their plantation, Primrose, is now called Warwick. Beauchamp was the family name of the father-in-law of the kingmaker of fifteenth-century England who had been Earl of Warwick before him. And Faulkner describes the aging Hubert as signing an I.O.U. to his nephew "Beauchamp" much as "the old proud earl himself might have scrawled Nevile" (and as Faulkner, himself, had annoyed Allen Tate by signing letters to the *Sewanee*

Review "Faulkner").[3] According to the revised genealogy, Tennie was the transmitter of the Beauchamp name from the white family which owned her to the black offspring of Carothers McCaslin when she married Turl, who "could have had any name he liked and no man would have cared, except the name his father bore who had no name."

Apart from Isaac McCaslin himself, the most important person in section four is his cousin, McCaslin Edmonds, a character, as I have noted, who had been newly conceived during the writing of the expanded version of "The Bear." Cass Edmonds opposes Ike in the long, rambling debate which makes up the major portion of section four, but their relationship, suggested by the way they are referred to, is such that they sometimes seem to be improvising plaintive arias in an operatic duet staged against the tainted and defeated South, "McCaslin" singing bass "and he" tenor, the two voices, if not suggesting two sides of Isaac McCaslin, certainly presenting two views that seemed to William Faulkner to possess truth. Carothers McCaslin Edmonds is sixteen years older than Isaac[4] but is one generation further removed from his namesake, Ike's grandfather, Lucius Quintus Carothers McCaslin. He has assumed Theophilus McCaslin's place in the family, having made the boy realize long before he reached twenty-one that he would never have to miss having a father. And when Faulkner revised "The Old People" and his first version of "The Bear," he naturally gave McCaslin the role that had been taken by the father in the discussions that concluded these stories. But much of McCaslin's argument in part four seems to contradict the father's role of moral preceptor in the earlier conversations, even though one of them is recalled in the midst of this discussion. Rather, in its moments of bitter skepticism at least, it is reminiscent of Mr. Compson's position in the dialogue Quentin imagines, or remembers, near the end of the second section of *The Sound and The Fury*. At other times McCaslin clearly speaks for Major de Spain, and General Compson, and for Faulkner himself, the Faulkner who returned again and again to Oxford, Mississippi, when a number of other southern writers, including many once extravagant praisers of the cultural values of the slaveholding South, have found it more convenient to live in the North; the Faulkner who operated a farm in Beat Two, Lafayette

County, and who would carefully identify himself as the descendant
of slaveholders in defending the southern position on desegregation
to a national audience in *Life*.[5] Something of the man whose legal
signature was William C. Falkner—great-grandson of William C.
Falkner, Confederate colonel and railroadbuilder, kindred spirit to
Collis Huntington and James J. Hill[6]—speaks when McCaslin opens
the discussion by replying to Isaac:

> "Relinquish. You, the direct male descendant of him who saw the opportunity
> and took it, bought the land, took the land, got the land no matter how, . . .
> out of the old grant, the first patent, when it was a wilderness of wild beasts
> and wilder men, and cleared it, translated it into something to bequeath to his
> children, worthy of bequeathment for his descendants' ease and security and
> pride and to perpetuate his name and accomplishments."

Although McCaslin Edmonds expresses some of Faulkner's
deepest feelings about the South, we identify primarily, in reading
section four, with Isaac McCaslin in his youthful attempt to shake
off the ancestral curse of slavery. Before McCaslin Edmonds is allowed his forceful words about old Carothers's accomplishments,
before we are even aware what the cousins are discussing in the
commissary, Faulkner anticipates the argument Isaac will later develop, when he writes in the opening paragraph that the grandfather
believed he had tamed and ordered the land and that he knew
better when he reared his descendants to think that the land was
his to hold and bequeath. The first words Isaac utters recall the
virginal spirit of the first version of "The Bear" and the social ideas
attributed to the McCaslin twins in *The Unvanquished*. He denies
that his grandfather ever owned the land to bequeath to his heirs
because, he argues, it could never be bought or sold since it was
made by the Creator for all to share, in the "communal anonymity
of brotherhood."[7] When his cousin, McCaslin, replies that Carothers
nevertheless did own it and that ever since man was disposessed of
Eden human society has been based upon the ownership of land
and the thralldom of men, Ike expounds a providential scheme of
history in which God, "dispossessed of Eden" by man, tolerated
man's ravishment of men in Europe and, ultimately, Ike's grandfather's ownership of the already tainted land in America because
He saw that grandfather would have the right descendants. "Maybe

He saw already in Grandfather the seed progenitive of the three generations He saw it would take to set at least some of His lowly people free."

Before we become fully aware of the young man's presumptuousness in making all human history culminate in himself as the emancipator, Faulkner has McCaslin call those lowly people "the sons of Ham." This leads to a discussion of the Bible's truth and of the human fallibility of its authors, who, Isaac maintains in remarks both reminiscent of the concluding discussion of the first "Bear" and anticipatory of the Nobel Prize speech and other public statements of Faulkner's last years, erred because they "were trying to write down the heart's truth out of the heart's driving complexity . . . of passion and lust and hate and fear." This portion of the argument ends with McCaslin surprisingly, if somewhat skeptically, willing to accept Isaac's belief that the "infallible and unerring heart" can know the simple and single truth of God. What brings about this momentary acceptance of the boy's argument is McCaslin's realization that all the descendants of old Carothers immediately recognized the wrong he did. McCaslin hopefully concludes by listing them. "Uncle Buck and Uncle Buddy. And they not the first and not alone. A thousand other Bucks and Buddies in less than two generations and sometimes less than one in this land which so you claim God created and man himself cursed and tainted."

When the conversation is picked up again after a twenty-one-page genealogical parenthesis, Isaac goes on to amplify his conception of the role he is to play as God's agent in redeeming the tainted land of the South. By this time we come to share some of the misgivings McCaslin expresses, and we may feel that McCaslin's acceptance of human evil is preferable to the boy's moral simplicity. But in the intervening pages as Ike glances up at the plantation ledgers on the shelf above the commissary desk and recalls learning what they contained, Faulkner compels us to work our way through the misspellings, to puzzle out what lies behind the written words, to share the boy's shock of discovery, to become one with him in this most deeply moving portion of the whole volume. The identification with Isaac established here, and in certain of the hunting sequences earlier, greatly affects the way we respond to other portions of section four and of "Delta Autumn" when Isaac's actions fall short of his ideals.

After Isaac is well into his recollections of reading the ledgers, Faulkner discloses that the reading took place when the boy was sixteen. He drops the phrase, "then he was sixteen," which recalls the emphatic "then he was twenty one" which had introduced the fourth section. The emphasis upon Ike's being sixteen associates his discovery of the family past with the deaths of Sam Fathers and the bear, which occurred in the same December; Faulkner further relates these deaths to the discovery of evil by stating that the boy "knew what he was going to find before he found it."

But the first entries he recalls constitute a hilarious, semiliterate running dialogue between his father, Buck, and his uncle, Buddy, about a slave named Percival Brownlee bought as a bookkeeper from the future general, Nathan Bedford Forrest, for $265 on March 3, 1856. The entry following the one recording Brownlee's purchase as a bookkeeper reads:

5 mar 1856 No bookepper any way Cant read. Can write his Name but I already put that down My self Says he can Plough but dont look like it to Me. sent to Feild to day Mar 5 1856

And another, also made by Buck:

6 Mar 1856 Cant plough either Says he aims to be a Precher so may be he can lead live stock to Crick to Drink

Buddy replies:

Mar 23th 1856 Cant do that either Except one at a Time Get shut of him

Buck's answer is:

24 Mar 1856 Who in hell would buy him

The sense of slavery conveyed is of something humorously innocuous, if rather inefficient; the tone is pretty much that of "Was" or of the early stories of *The Unvanquished*.

The tone changes dramatically as Isaac moves on through the ledgers. He reads of Roscius and Phoebe, the old family slaves, who

had been brought along from Carolina to Mississippi and who refused to leave the plantation when they were freed in his grandfather's will. The first notation to suggest anything disturbing in the
relations between the McCaslins and their Negroes concerns:

Thucydus Roskus @ Fibby Son born in Callina 1779. Refused 10acre peace
fathers Will 28 Jun 1837 Refused Cash offer $200. dolars from A.@ T.
McCaslin 28 Jun 1837 Wants to stay and work it out

The record of that process which covered five pages and almost five
years of the ledgers—the wages paid and the charges made against
them for molasses, meat, and meal and for shoes and, now and then,
for a coat to keep out the cold and rain—caused Ike to sense what
it meant to be the black man "entering the commissary, asking permission perhaps of the white man's son to see the ledger-page
which he could not even read, not even asking for the white man's
word, which he would have had to accept for the reason that there
was absolutely no way under the sun for him to test it, as to how
the account stood."

For the moment Isaac seems unconcerned with the reason
behind Thucydides' refusal of his legacy from Carothers McCaslin
and his insistence on working for the two hundred dollars. But the
reason is disclosed almost immediately. After the final entry on
Thucydides comes this one written by Buck:

Eunice Bought by Father in New Orleans 1807 $650. dolars. Marrid to
Thucydus 1809 Drownd in Crick Cristmas Day 1832

Buddy then wrote:

June 21th 1833 Drownd herself

and Buck:

23 Jun 1833 Who in hell ever heard of a niger drownding him self

and Buddy replied:

Aug 13th 1833 Drownd herself

"And he thought *But why? But why?* He was sixteen then." The staccato force of the repetitions of "Drownd herself" pounds our consciousness as we read as powerfully as they did Isaac's. He proceeds to an entry concerning *"Tomasina called Tomy Daughter of Thucydus @ Eunice"* who died in childbed, and then to one concerning her son Terrel:

Turl Son of Thucydus @ Eunice Tomy born Jun 1833 yr stars fell Fathers will

What hits Ike here is "Fathers will." The leaving, without explanation, of a thousand dollars to the son of an unmarried slave, to be paid when the boy came of age. *"I reckon that was cheaper than saying My son to a nigger,"* he says to himself bitterly. But he tries to find some way to justify his grandfather. *"But there must have been love,"* he thinks. *"Some sort of love."* He imagines the old man, a widower, alone in the house, sending for the girl out of loneliness, to have someone young and lively about him. Then he attempts to understand the feelings of Tomey's parents in first sending her, thinks of them considering themselves above the field slaves, the husband "inherited by the white man from his father, and the white man himself had travelled three hundred miles and better to New Orleans in a day when men travelled by horseback or steamboat, and bought the girl's mother as wife for   and that was all." His effort somehow to absolve his grandfather collapses when he comes to understand what Carothers had been after in New Orleans, when the significance of the entry recording Eunice's being bought in 1807 but not married to Thucydides until 1809 breaks upon him. He thinks, *"His own daughter   His own daughter   No No Not even him."* Then Ike's mind returns to the mother's feelings, the feelings of Eunice who Uncle Buddy had been certain had "Drownd herself," and he imagines her walking into the icy creek fifty years earlier, "six months before her daughter's and her lover's (*Her first lover's* he [thinks]. *Her first*) child was born, solitary, inflexible, griefless, ceremonial, in formal and succinct repudiation of grief and despair who had already had to repudiate belief and hope"

At this point Faulkner writes for the second time, "That was all," a phrase he repeats like a refrain three more times in the next eleven pages. Once the full horror of Carothers McCaslin's ownership of Eunice has been revealed, Isaac passes on to the entries concerning Tennie Beauchamp and her children. One function of the ledger entries is to link the other stories of *Go Down, Moses* to "The Bear." And the earlier stories take on a retrospective poignancy from the information disclosed. "Was" is never the same after it has become clear that Turl is, equally with the twins, a son of Carothers McCaslin. Knowing more of Lucas's family history does not make any great difference to us because his nature has been pretty fully delineated earlier, but Tennie's Jim suddenly becomes a much more interesting figure after the following entries have been read:

James Thucydus Beauchamp Son of Tomes Turl and Tenny Beauchamp Born 29th december 1864 and both Well Wanted to call him Theophilus but Tride Amodeus McCaslin and Callina McCaslin and both dide so Disswaded Them Born at Two clock A,m, both Well

Vanished sometime on night of his twenty-first birthday Dec 29 1885. Traced by Isaac McCaslin to Jackson Tenn. and there lost. His third of legacy $1000.00 returned to McCaslin Edmonds Trustee this day Jan 12 1886

The first of these entries is one written by Uncle Buddy and recalled by Isaac from his reading that December after the final hunt. In the second, Faulkner moves ahead to an entry made over two years later by Isaac himself. By becoming, like his father and uncle, an author of the family chronicles and by getting involved in the dispensing of the legacies of his black first cousins, Isaac has come to share in his family's heritage more fully than he realizes.

From this point on in section four, Faulkner begins to move freely forward and back in time as it suits his purpose, limiting himself less and less to the discussion and Isaac's memories of reading the ledgers. But as time becomes more fluid, we become more and more aware of concrete moments of time and of specific dates. Neither the first three sections of "The Bear" nor the stories written earlier had mentioned dates. We got only a general sense of the period in which the action took place, whether contemporary or of the times preceding or following the Civil War. But once Faulkner begins to provide particular dates in the ledgers, we are driven to become our own genealogists and historians, to deduce birth and death dates which are not supplied, to place precisely in time crucial events like the hunt for the bear and the argument over Isaac's inheritance. Faulkner unobstrusively supplies some of the key dates, but these only whet our appetite for more.

After the entries devoted to Tennie's Jim, Faulkner gives us two others, a final one written by Theophilus McCaslin:

Miss sophonsiba b dtr t t @ t 1869

and one, which Isaac might have written but never felt the need to:

Lucas Quintus Carothers McCaslin Beauchamp. Last surviving son and child of Tomey's Terrel and Tennie Beauchamp. March 17, 1874

In 1886 Fonsiba married a northern black with a grant from the federal government for a farm in Arkansas.[8] The account of Isaac's trip through December mud and rain to distribute her third of the legacy is one of the most powerfully written passages in *Go Down, Moses*, and it should not be forgotten when the discussion of Isaac's refusal of his inheritance is resumed one page after the trip is completed. After days of lonely and desperate travel by rail, contracted stage, hired livery rig, rail again, and finally by horse, he locates the log house "with a clay chimney which seemed in process of being flattened by the rain to a nameless and valueless rubble of dissolution in that roadless and even pathless waste of unfenced fallow and wilderness jungle—no barn, no stable, not so much as a hen coop." Inside in fireless gloom he finds the husband in ministerial clothes reading a book with gold-framed, but lensless, spectacles. Distressed by the incompetence and folly he sees all about him, Isaac returns to the theme of the curse on the land he had developed in the earlier argument with his cousin. "Dont you see? This whole land, the whole South, is cursed, and all of us who derive from it." In the earlier discussion the young man had been essentially optimistic, full of faith in God's providence and in his own place in it. Here his tone has changed. In reply to Fonsiba's husband's announcing that they have entered a new era dedicated to "freedom, liberty, and equality for all, to which this country will be the new Canaan," he asks, "Freedom from what? From work? Canaan?" And with a gesture summoning up the fields unplowed and empty of stock, which anticipates similar gestures McCaslin Edmonds will make when the argument is resumed, he demands, "What corner of Canaan is this?" To his sense Fonsiba seems totally alien as she cowers against the wall; only her fathomless eyes, watching from a coffee-colored face "without alarm, without recognition, without hope," appear alive. In reply to his concern for her welfare, she declares pathetically, "I'm free."

After supplying the imaginary ledger entry which might have been written recording Lucas's birth, Faulkner moves on to the scene in which Lucas demands on his twenty-first birthday, in 1895, the rest of the money remaining from old Carothers's will. This carries the action seven years beyond the time of the conversation between Isaac and his cousin, McCaslin (which Faulkner presently takes up again after the twenty-one-page interruption), and allows him to provide a glimpse into Isaac's future married life. This view ahead, which is also concerned with the possibility of freedom, should warn us against too easy acceptance of arguments in the pages that follow. The passage, punctuated before and after with the final reassertions of "That was all," begins:

1874 the boy; 1888 the man, repudiated denied and free; 1895 and husband but no father, unwidowered but without a wife, and found long since that no man is ever free and probably could not bear it if he were; married then and living in Jefferson in the little new jerrybuilt bungalow which his wife's father had given them:

Then after a brief account of Lucas's demanding "the rest of that money old Carothers left," the discussion in the commissary is resumed at the point it left off, with McCaslin still speaking of southerners like Buck and Buddy doing their best to "fumble-heed that truth so mazed for them that spoke it and so confused for them that heard." Ike replies that Bucks and Buddies are not enough, and he is beginning to develop his notion of his own role in God's plan, thinking of himself this time as a second Old Testament Isaac instead of a redeemer, "fatherless and therefore safe," repudiating being sacrificed because this time the exasperated God might not intervene and substitute the kid, when McCaslin suddenly breaks in, muttering, "Escape." Seeming to accept this comment on his intended renunciation, Isaac resumes his discourse as if he had not been interrupted. But he does attempt to clarify his position as he proceeds. Modifying his conception of God from that advanced in earlier stages of the discussion, of One all-knowing if not all-powerful, to One who is dependent on human action, he describes Him as looking for the last time helplessly and without hope at the rich and fertile South and the whole hopeful continent beyond it to the north and west, ready to abandon it all until He became aware of "one simple enough to believe that horror and outrage were first and last simply horror and outrage and . . . crude enough to act upon that." The action Isaac has in mind, which caused God to turn once again to this land, was his own action of taking down the ancestral musket, with the apparent intention of doing something against the "horror and the outrage."

Perhaps because he is moved by his kinsman's youthful earnestness, McCaslin foregoes making any personal challenge here. He questions neither Isaac's sense of himself nor the value of the action he describes—which ultimately does not lead to his challenging the South's racial and moral difficulties, as the youth suggests, but rather foreshadows the man's retreat from them into the simpler worlds of carpentry and hunting. Instead McCaslin merely expresses skepticism of the idea that God is turning once again to the South. And almost immediately the skepticism dissolves, and his voice rises to join his young cousin's in an antiphonal chorus, recounting the ways in which the war served God's ultimate purposes. The agreement of these cousins becomes complete after a time, and Faulkner's own voice takes over the narration from McCaslin, telling of the South during the Reconstruction and after, of things seen by Cass and inherited by Isaac.

This providential conception of the Civil War attributed to Mississippi cousins conversing in the old commissary of the plantation in 1888, with its emphasis on accidental calamities visited upon the South, is reminiscent of actual theories of the 1860s, and these passages contain some bravura strokes of Faulkner's narrative imagination, extravagant and wonderfully compelling: the ex-slave bootlegger become U.S. marshal, named Sickymo from the Sycamore tree under which he had cached his pints; later glimpses of the effeminate Percival Brownlee, passing through the square in Jefferson in 1866 in the entourage of a federal army paymaster and, finally, old and fat, the owner of a fancy brothel in New Orleans. But the discourse becomes garrulous and self-indulgent as Isaac and McCaslin and then Faulkner take turns recalling the war and its aftermath. Ike describes southern women nursing ailing slaves in their company rooms, and his cousin and he join in recalling the gallantry of the men. Faulkner's voice provides no check to the self-indulgence of this history but manages, with some deft chronological sleight of hand, to pass over the original Ku Klux Klan and attribute the revived Klan to the grandsons of Union Army camp followers.

It seems unlikely that Faulkner expected this mock history to be taken totally seriously. As the historical discussion rambles on for several pages, most of us are likely to become detached, to lose our intense involvement with Isaac McCaslin, and to take his providential conception of history much less seriously after it has been mixed with traditional Confederate pieties. But Faulkner eventually brings the historical discussion back into focus on the specific realities of the McCaslin family, as Cass gestures toward the desk where new ledgers had been filled recording the chronicle of the land and its races in the years since emancipation. The narrative regains emotional force as Faulkner mentions the old names, Turl now dead and Jim and Fonsiba gone and only Lucas left. But the system has continued, modified only slightly; there are new names to replace the old, more men and women bound by the ledgers "to the land their sweat fell on."

As the discussion swings back to the ledgers, McCaslin, who had taken over the running of the farm after the war, becomes the voice of some of Faulkner's deepest feelings about the fate of being a white southerner. Isaac reopens the dialogue by denying that the new bondage will last forever. He sees it as something tolerated against his will by God, but something which is all right because the blacks, as Faulkner would write a few years later about Dilsey, endure. In going on to say that they are better than the whites, Isaac falters. Faulkner explains that "even in the act of escaping (and maybe this was the reality and truth of his need to escape)" he knew that this was heresy, that even in fleeing from his southern heritage he was taking more of his unregenerate old grandfather with him than "even he had feared." The falter anticipates the old man Isaac was destined to become, the Uncle Ike already conceived in "Delta Autumn," but the idealistic argument recalls the boy hunter of the first version of "The Bear." In the face of

McCaslin's renewed teasing and skepticism, Isaac declares that the vices of the blacks are aped from white men or bred by the conditions of slavery, but that their virtues are their own: "Endurance . . . and pity and tolerance and forebearance and fidelity and love of children . . . and more." These, he argues, they got not from the whites but "from the old free fathers a longer time free than us because we have never been free."

Twenty-one-year-old Ike looks over at his apparently hard-bitten cousin and notices in his eyes a look he remembers from seven years earlier. And at this point Faulkner brings the moral world of Sam Fathers and the virgin woods into the shoe-scuffed commissary which he had described as squatting like a portent over the tainted cotton fields worked by black slaves and tenants for the whites who owned them. He inserts and italicizes the conversation that had concluded the first version of "The Bear,"[9] which had been omitted from its chronological place in the second section of the story in *Go Down, Moses*, the discussion of the boy's refraining from shooting the bear and instead rushing in to pull the fyce from beneath his towering bulk. The significance of this conversation, in which the boy's father, here replaced by McCaslin, had used Keats's "Ode on a Grecian Urn" to explain the moral importance of abstaining from killing, had been unambiguous. But its meaning is more complex in its new setting at the culmination of the long dialogue between the cousins.

Seven years before, McCaslin had been the mentor, and the boy now recalls his concluding words: "Courage and honor and pride, and pity and love of justice and of liberty. They all touch the heart, and what the heart holds to become truth, as far as we know truth." Isaac and Cass had then been of one mind, united by these words. This time they are both united and divided by their memories of them. Ike's whole argument has been based on the conviction that the moral truths of the wilderness can and must be applied to human society. McCaslin, sixteen years older, is certain that nothing that simple can ever be done. In part because he also knows what the ledgers contain, he refuses, except momentarily, to allow himself to share the boy's moral optimism. He is guarded and skeptical, often a little bitter, sobered by an awareness of human weaknesses and by a strong sense of the weight of the past.

After having been the listener during great stretches of the earlier part of the conversation, he now attempts to resume the role of teacher he had had seven years earlier, to confute the moral simplicity of his young cousin. He begins by pretending to concede that the land is cursed as the boy has argued and raises his hand to suggest all that is involved, the whole social fabric of the plantation that survived the war and has even increased in size and which will last as long as he "and his McCaslin successors lasted." Then, after Isaac shifts the burden of the curse from the land to the McCaslins themselves, he insists that the inheritance, however soiled, descends to "the third generation too, and the male, the eldest, the direct and sole and white and still McCaslin even, father to son to son."

McCaslin's view, conservative, socially rooted rather than individualistic, seems almost European. Americans can rarely bring themselves to take history seriously, to believe really that what they are and what they will be have been significantly limited by their past, by their family, by their place in the social order, and by the region in which they were born. Isaac's belief that he can cast off his heritage seems characteristically American. His renouncing the McCaslin land and all it involves recalls Huckleberry Finn's lighting out for the Territory to avoid being civilized. Both youths flee the complexities of human society to gain an idealized independence. Huck sought his freedom in the unsettled land to the west, but Isaac's refuge is, in a sense, in the past. His relation to the past is ambiguous. At the same time that he believes he has freed himself from his particular, tainted, ancestral past, he wishes to regain another past, ideal, primitive, Eden-like, to live as a hunter and carpenter. He longs for a life of prehistorical Arcadian simplicity like that of the "old free fathers," in which he can escape from the moral complexities of the tamed and ravaged land of the postwar South.

McCaslin denies the possibility of escape from the morally ambiguous present and from the past that produced it. In answer to Isaac's declaring himself freed from the ancestral burden of racial injustice, he insists, "No, not now nor ever, we from them nor they from us." He then goes on to explain that he too would repudiate the inheritance if he could. "Even you can see that I could do no

else." But it is impossible. "I am what I am; I will always be what
I was born and have always been."

Faulkner allows Isaac to have the concluding words in the long,
tangled discussion: "Yes. Sam Fathers set me free." But they do not
constitute the last word in the argument. The next two episodes,
which bring section four to a conclusion—not to mention the already
written "Delta Autumn"—provide ironic commentary on Isaac
McCaslin's youthful faith. The first of these episodes is the story of
another legacy, that from Uncle Hubert Beauchamp, a shiny tin
coffeepot. This tall tale, told in the carefree spirit of "Was," relieves
the intensity built up during the extended dialogue. The legacy was
no scrawled sentence in a will but a thing, originally a silver loving
cup ceremonially filled with fifty gold coins and sealed in a burlap
package. As a child, Isaac had noticed changes in Warwick, his
uncle's shabby, paintless mansion, the inside each time seeming
larger, as the furnishings gradually disappeared. And once he had
witnessed the routing of a mulatto mistress who retreated in a "once-
hooped dress ballooning and flapping below a man's overcoat."
Changes in his uncle's way of life—which culminated in a twenty-
two-mile trip to the McCaslin place, after the almost empty Warwick
burned, riding doubled up on an old white mare with Tennie's great-
grandfather—were accompanied by changes in the weight, sound,
and, eventually, the shape of the burlap package. And then when
"he was twenty one," in McCaslin's presence, apparently an hour or
two after the discussion of the other inheritance, Isaac Beauchamp
McCaslin cut open the package on the dining room table and found
in the brand-new coffeepot only a handful of coppers and "a collection of minutely-folded scraps of paper sufficient almost for a
rat's nest." These slips, a series of I.O.U.'s written on paper beginning with good linen bond and concluding in newspaper margins
and an overall label, constitute a history in small of the disintegra-
tion of the hopes of the Old South. Of the longest one,

I.O.U. Beauchamp McCaslin[10] *or his heirs twenty-five (25) pieces Gold This &*
All preceeding constituting My notes of hand at twenty (20) percentum com-
pounded annually. This date of 19th January 1873

                                                Beauchamp

Faulkner wryly writes, "What dream, what dreamed splendid recoup, not of any injury or betrayal of trust because it had been merely a loan: nay, a partnership."

Once again the reactions of the cousins are contrasted. McCaslin, who spoke up for the accomplishments of old Carothers and took a guardedly hopeful attitude toward the South in the earlier conversation, now stands back from the table "intolerant and repudiating" as the burlap is opened, and then grumbles, "So you have plenty of coppers anyway." Isaac doesn't even hear his cousin but, lost in thought, looks peacefully at the tin pot. In the brief period since the discussion of the other legacy, he has become mature enough to survey this record of human weakness and defeat with equanimity. He accepts as a loan money from his inheritance which McCaslin forces on him, and curbs his earlier tendency to take himself solemnly with a touch of ironic humor, musing about

how much it takes to compound a man (Isaac McCaslin for instance) and of the devious intricate choosing yet unerring path that man's (Isaac McCaslin's for instance) spirit takes among all that mass to make him at last what he is to be, not only the astonishment of them (the ones who sired the McCaslin who sired his father and Uncle Buddy and their sister, and the ones who sired the Beauchamp who sired his Uncle Hubert and his Uncle Hubert's sister) who believed they had shaped him, but to Isaac McCaslin too.

After describing the legacy from Uncle Hubert and telling of Isaac's taking up the carpenter's trade, Faulkner concludes the fourth section of "The Bear" with an account of Isaac's marriage, his third inheritance. At first, he achieved with his wife a state of grace like that he had achieved alone in the wilderness. It was a new country, "out of the earth, beyond the earth yet of the earth," his heritage and the heritage of all who shared together and by sharing became one. But the shining new country is soon corroded by his wife's desire that they have the ancestral land. In a grotesque and melodramatic scene Isaac succumbs to her sexual temptation and agrees, momentarily, to reclaim it. So the fourth section—which began with a boy's renunciation of a tainted heritage because he believed that freed from it he could redeem the South from racial injustice, and included a man's compassionate acceptance of another legacy, the worthless product of well-intentioned folly—concludes with a young husband's thinking of his recently acquired wife, "She *is lost. She was born lost. We were all born lost.*" And the wife, laughing hysterically, apparently realizing that Isaac will repudiate his agreement, sounds again, one final time the theme, "That was all," declaring, "And that's all. That's all from me. If this dont get you that son you talk about, it wont be mine."

CHAPTER SIX

THE CONCLUDING SECTION

SAVE FOR THE GLIMPSE we get of Isaac McCaslin's breakfast table on the morning of Lucas Beauchamp's twenty-first birthday in 1895, the view of Isaac presented at the end of section four—a "husband but no father, unwidowered but without a wife," harshly awakened from his dream of freeing himself from human evil—is in the chronological sequence of his life the last which Faulkner provides us until he appears as a very old man in "Delta Autumn." In the concluding section of "The Bear," Faulkner takes us back in time to the June three years before Isaac's coming of age in order to describe his final trip back to Big Bottom before the lumber company got to the timber. This section, though placed earlier in chronological time than "Delta Autumn" and the fourth section of "The Bear" and placed in the book before "Delta Autumn"[1] and the story, "Go Down, Moses," is in some ways the true culmination of the history of Isaac McCaslin.

At least since Sartre's essay of 1939 explaining the handling of time in *The Sound and the Fury*,[2] readers have been alert to the effects Faulkner achieves through interrupting the steady movement of chronological time, dissolving the present in memories of the past. The treatment of time in "The Bear" differs from that in the great early novels because the future as well as the past is made to break in on the present. The most careful study of time in the story is in the essay R. W. B. Lewis included in *The Picaresque Saint*. Lewis points out that "The Bear" begins when Isaac McCaslin is sixteen, slips quickly back into his childhood, and then moves back to his sixteenth year for the fateful events of the last hunt. Time meanders back and forward and yet seems not to move at all. Everything, in a sense, occurs simultaneously in the three opening sections. As Charles Mallison was to perceive in *Intruder in the Dust,* "Yesterday today and tomorrow are Is: Indivisible."[3] And time continues to be "Is" in the fourth section of "The Bear." Here the main current of time begins at Isaac's twenty-first birthday with the argument over the inheritance, and then eddies back into the family past, to his own birth and beyond as he recalls reading the plantation ledgers at sixteen. Later time moves back up to his twenty-first birthday and then on a year or two into his early married life. But in addition to the principal movement, there are lesser drifts of time. These are in part intrusions from the future.

Sartre found the view of life presented in Faulkner's early works too bleak to be valid. He considered the novels, despite their great power, untrue to life because they lacked any awareness of a relationship between the past and a future. In Sartre's view Faulkner's present appeared without reason, "like a thief," and then dissolved leaving nothing because there was no sense of progression, no hint of what Martin Heidegger called "the silent strength of the possible." Protagonists of the earlier novels often seemed incapacitated by an enormous weight of the past in a universe without any real future.

This is to some extent changed in *Go Down, Moses*, but there is no immensely great possibility of hope. It is hard to conceive of anyone with a greater faith in the possibilities of the future than the twenty-one-year-old Isaac McCaslin, upholding his beliefs against the unillusioned pessimism of his older cousin. Isaac's sense of human capability is too hopeful for even the Faulkner of 1941, a Faulkner whose conception of life had mellowed considerably since he had written the great novels from *The Sound and the Fury* through *Absalom, Absalom!* While the young man explains to his cousin his dream of a future free of inherited evil, Faulkner is careful to provide us with glimpses into the future which lies before him. And these suggestions of Isaac McCaslin's future are nearly as discouraging as the memories of the past which had crippled many of the protagonists of Faulkner's earlier books. The future for Isaac could contain little hope because it had already been determined. Young Isaac's future is limited by the Uncle Ike he is to become, the old, discouraged man Faulkner had already described in writing "Delta Autumn." In the total context of *Go Down, Moses*, in which "Delta Autumn" serves as an epilogue to "The Bear," Isaac's hopefulness about the future makes section four the least hopeful of the divisions of the greater story.

Against the pessimism of the fourth section and of "Delta Autumn," Faulkner set the account of Ike McCaslin's return to the wilderness in the second June following the last hunt. The fifth section is given special emphasis by being placed out of its normal chronological position. Narrative order is always more significant than mere chronology in Faulkner's works, and the magnificent fifth section has the additional importance of being, save for final revisions of "Delta Autumn," the portion of the life of Isaac McCaslin which Faulkner in all probability wrote last. Yet the trip back to the big woods is based on something he had written as early as 1935, the trip taken by the young narrator, "Quentin," in the concluding part of "Lion," the earliest of the major hunting stories. Faulkner's transformations of this portion of "Lion" to make it into the final section of "The Bear" are of considerable interest, as that section reflects all that has gone before and provides the definitive portrait of Isaac McCaslin.

In "Lion" the conclusion was explicitly an account of the way the death of the heroic dog affected the "two people who loved him most," Major de Spain and Boon Hogganbeck. Comparatively little was made of the youthful Quentin's own reaction to that death. The boy's visit to Major de Spain, who declined his invitation to go with him and who never did return to the woods, is substantially the same in both versions. Taking a log train into the woods, Quentin meets Ad (Ash in "The Bear") and is told, in heavy Negro dialect, that Boon got in the night before and has been hunting since before daylight near a gum tree in an old clearing. As an afterthought, Ad warns of snakes. "Dey's crawling now." Once in the thick greenness of the woods, the boy realizes that they seem different and that the difference is not simply that they are now the summer woods. He realizes, even he, "a boy, who had owned no Lion," why Major de Spain could never return. He passes Lion's grave, which has been obliterated by a spring flood, and thinks that this is all right "because it was not Lion who was there." The closest approach to the mood of the final section of "The Bear" comes when the boy, musing over the deaths of Lion and Old Ben, concludes that perhaps they are better off after "the long challenge and the long chase, the one with no heart to be driven and outraged, the other with no flesh to be mauled and bled." From the grave site he moves through heat and mosquitoes toward the gum tree and becomes aware of a furious hammering of metal on metal. Then he comes in sight of Boon sitting under the tree, which is full of terrified squirrels, pounding at one part of his gun with the rest of it scattered around him.

In "Lion" Faulkner clearly explains the significance of the last furious and futile tableau. Boon's behavior is contrasted with the restrained mourning of Major de Spain. Quentin tells us that Boon was "living, as always in the moment; nothing on earth—not Lion— not anything in the past—mattered to him except his helpless fury with his broken gun." Without stopping or looking up to see who has arrived, he shouts, roughly and desperately, to the boy to get away and leave the squirrels alone. "They're mine!"[4]

The transformation of Quentin's return to the woods where Lion had died into the culminating experience in the life of Isaac McCaslin was primarily accomplished by adding material. In the fifteen pages of the fifth section of "The Bear," Faulkner retained with little essential modification almost everything in the two double-column pages devoted to the episode in *Harper's* except two passages explaining its significance. These were discarded because they related everything to the death of Lion, but Faulkner provided no comparable explanations in "The Bear." We have to make out as best we can for ourselves the meaning of Boon's behavior at the end of the story.

Faulkner made little of the log train in "Lion" or in the earlier parts of "The Bear." It was simply a convenient means of getting in or out of the woods. But in working on the final section of "The Bear," he wished to give concrete embodiment to the spiritual loss associated with the deaths of Sam Fathers and Old Ben. Therefore he moved the physical destruction of the wilderness, so overwhelming in "Delta Autumn," back into the 1880s and had Major de Spain sell the timber rights on the hunting grounds to a lumber company.[5] Once he had decided to portray the wilderness under threat of imminent destruction, Faulkner saw the full potentiality of the train as emblem of the new age of mechanical exploitation of nature, as precursor of the mile-long freights that howled across the treeless plain in "Delta Autumn." He writes of it as harmless once but no longer. It had always seemed like a child's toy to the hunters, sounding its insignificant whistle and sending up miniature puffs of smoke as it rushed incessantly along, never seeming to get anywhere in the inattentive immensity of the wilderness. On its first trip—this delightful tall tale was, according to Faulkner's brother John, based on an actual incident[6]—it so startled a half-grown bear from perusing "the curious symmetrical squared barkless logs" placed in an unending geometrical line that the animal scrambled up a young ash and cowered there, face hidden in its paws, and remained nearly thirty-six hours. But on Isaac's return to the woods, the train no longer seemed a charming toy. As it moved off from Hoke's, he thought that instead it looked like a little dingy snake disappearing into the weeds.

Much of the emphasis in the concluding part of "Lion" had been upon the reactions of Major de Spain and Boon to the fatal consequences of the last hunt. In "The Bear" almost everything is related to Isaac McCaslin's own feelings. At first, he is troubled by a sense that things are not the same and can never be the same again. He realizes that the woods are doomed and feels that both the once harmless train and he himself bring with them a premonition of the half-finished planing mill he had tried to avoid seeing at the log line junction. But once the train has gone and he has met Ash and moved on foot into the woods, they again seem impervious to time and change, and he can look back with indulgence as he recalls the old Negro's envious and wildly inept effort to be a hunter six years earlier on the day after he had killed his first deer—a day on which the hunters were back at home, according to "The Old People."

Faulkner's prose takes on a grave and measured eloquence as it celebrates the immortality of the natural world and the mortality of all things human. Enclosed in the green solitude of the summer woods, Isaac McCaslin realizes that the changing seasons are changeless, "summer, and fall, and snow, and wet and saprife spring in their ordered immortal sequence." These were "the deathless and immemorial phases of the mother who had shaped him if any had toward the man he almost was." But there was also the old man "who had been his spirit's father if any had, whom he had revered and harkened to and loved and lost and grieved." And in addition— and here Faulkner once again moves forward in time in order to glance back at a past most dear in being lost—there was his marriage and brief possession of the "unsubstanced glory which inherently of itself cannot last and hence why glory"; yet he "would, might, carry even the remembrance of it into the time when flesh no longer talks to flesh because memory at least does last."

Isaac's effortlessly finding the tin containing Old Ben's paw buried in the unmarked grave of Lion is a final confirmation of his woodcraft, a feat reminiscent of his abandoning his gun, watch, and compass to earn a rendezvous with the bear in section one. In "Lion" the young narrator had become reconciled to the deaths of the great dog and the old bear because he sensed that they had at last found relief from the torments of life, from "the long challenge and the long chase." In "The Bear" the elegy becomes a hymn of affirmation. After Isaac finds the tin, which he had left full of burial offerings, rusted and empty, he fills another nailed to a tree with more symbolic gifts for Sam, a twist of tobacco, a bandana handkerchief, and some peppermint candy. They disappear almost before he has turned away, and Faulkner writes that they had "not vanished but merely translated into the myriad life which printed the dark mold of these secret and sunless places with delicate fairy tracks." At this moment the boy becomes convinced that death has no lasting reality, that men and animals live on in the wild things of nature. This belief, which recalls the natural religion of Whitman, and which was first suggested in the discussion which concludes "The Old People," is rendered with a somber majesty beyond anything else in American literature. Faulkner describes Ike leaving the grave knoll

which was no abode of the dead because there was no death, not Lion and not Sam: not held fast in earth but free in earth and not in earth but of earth, myriad yet undiffused of every myriad part, leaf and twig and particle, air and sun and rain and dew and night, acorn oak and leaf and acorn again, dark and dawn and dark and dawn again in their immutable progression and, being myriad, one: and Old Ben too, Old Ben too.

But Isaac's meditation on earthly immortality is broken by the sudden presence at his knee of a rattlesnake. His response to this mortal threat is fear but not fright, recalling and reversing Sam's earlier counsel, "Be scared . . . . But dont be afraid." The snake is old, with its once-bright coloring dulled "to a monotone concordant . . . with the wilderness it crawled and lurked." It seems to the boy "the old one, the ancient and accursed about the earth, fatal and solitary," and he smells not only the sick stink of rotting cucumbers but something more "which had no name, evocative of all knowledge and an old weariness and of pariah-hood and of death." But as the snake begins to glide solemnly away, he salutes it in the tongue of the old fathers as Sam had saluted the mysterious buck, calling it "Chief, . . . Grandfather."

In "Lion," Ad had warned the boy that snakes were crawling, but he had met none. From that hint of serpents in a wilderness world which had lapsed from the heroic age of the great dog and the old bear, Faulkner developed the snake that materialized as Isaac moved from the grave knoll toward the gum tree where Boon hammered at his gun. As the recalling of Sam Fathers's salutation suggests, Faulkner expected this moment in "The Bear" to be related to the conclusion of "The Old People." Another antecedent that Faulkner probably had in mind in conceiving the snake is the cottonmouth moccasin that slashed the black man fleeing for his life before Indian pursuers in the great early story "Red Leaves." The black fugitive addressed the moccasin, "Olé, grandfather." Sam Fathers had spoken in celebration of the immortal spirits of his people, which still lived, in other forms, in the natural world. The fugitive black's address was an expression of his sense of death; it immediately preceded his recognition of how greatly he wished not to die. Isaac McCaslin's valediction to the snake incorporates something of the feelings of both the black and Sam. Isaac's using the word grandfather suggests his evil grandfather, old Carothers McCaslin. But the suggestiveness of the snake cannot be limited to anything so specific. Faulkner's description seems to relate it to the biblical serpent in the garden which led Eve to a tree of knowledge of good and evil and brought death to us all.

In section four Ike had rejected his inheritance from old Carothers. He declined to be another Isaac sacrificed at the familial altar and argued that he had been freed of the ancestral curse by Sam Fathers. Now—three years earlier in chronological time but later in the time of narration and, in all likelihood, in Faulkner's order in writing—he accepts the serpent and salutes it. This action marks his true coming of age, his acceptance of what it means to be a man.

To turn from society to the wilderness might seem to be to flee from the complexities of human life. That is what Isaac had attempted to do in section four when he argued that the only hope of salvation for the South, and for himself, lay in his renunciation. But in the concluding section the wilderness is not a virginal retreat free from the complications of ordinary living. Throughout "The Bear," the woods themselves have been presented in a continuously changing light. Their evolution has paralleled that of Isaac McCaslin. In the opening section, as in the earlier version of the story, the wilderness is immense, mysterious, entirely without taint. It provides a setting for the immortal bear and the ageless descendant of Indian chiefs, who effect the moral tuition of the boy. Later it becomes the tragic theater in which the boy participates in the fated drama that culminates in the deaths of the great bear and the old man. In the final section the wilderness is doomed and at the same time beyond all mortality. It is permeated with memories of Sam and Old Ben and the brave dog Lion. From almost the beginning of the story it has contained the threat of death, and now it includes both primal and specific evil, the snake that crawls within its precincts suggesting, on the one hand, the evil one himself, and on the other, Carothers McCaslin. In a sense the wilderness comes to incorporate the tamed land of the fourth section and its racial injustice.

Isaac's recognition of the serpent that lurks in the wilderness is not a lapse into moral indifference. He salutes it not because he has forgotten Eunice and Tennie's Jim and the teachings of Sam Fathers, but because he has gained an awareness of human limitations. Like the earlier rendezvous with the bear, which marked the boy's achieving of virtue, this confrontation is of transcendent importance. By saluting the snake, Isaac shows that he understands what his cousin, McCaslin, had been trying to tell him when he said that he could be only what he was born and what he had always been. He now realizes that no man can ever be wholly free. Having shed his youthful illusions of redeeming the South from evil through personal renunciation, and being still unencumbered by the bitterness which was to sour his old age in "Delta Autumn," Isaac McCaslin has attained a wise and tragic understanding that to be fully human is to be contaminated with evil and, ultimately, to die.

PART THREE

Changes Following "The Bear"

CHAPTER SEVEN

"THE OLD PEOPLE" AND "WAS"

ONCE FAULKNER HAD worked out the genealogical connections between the McCaslins and the family of Lucas Beauchamp and decided to make "The Bear" the keystone of a book which would include several of his recent stories, he sensed that many of the stories would have to be revised. The amount of revision he found necessary to adapt the earlier pieces to the genealogical plan and the powerful themes of "The Bear" varied greatly from story to story. And even in their final, revised forms the diverse segments of *Go Down, Moses* never quite fused into a seamless whole; discrepancies remain, evidence of the piecemeal making and subsequent patching of the structure.

Of the six published[1] and two unpublished stories which Faulkner put together with "The Bear," three—"Gold Is Not Always," "Pantaloon in Black," and "Go Down, Moses"—were not substantially altered. Changes in the *Harper's* version of "The Old People" and in the unpublished story "Was" were limited pretty much to shifting the point of view of the narration from the first person and altering the names of characters to relate the happenings to the life history of Isaac McCaslin. In "Was" the nine-year-old Bayard Sartoris was replaced as the child observer by Isaac's cousin McCaslin Edmonds, and the owners of Tennie, Jason and Sophonsiba Prim, were renamed Beauchamp. When Faulkner revised "The Old People," he put Isaac McCaslin into the story in the role of the boy protagonist as he had already done in his retrospective glance at the events of this story in "Delta Autumn." In the discussion of the meaning of the ghostly buck's appearance that concludes "The Old People," he replaced the boy's father with McCaslin Edmonds. Another change was the renaming of Jimbo. He was called Tennie's Jim, the same name he had in both versions of "The Bear."

In addition to the adjustments in the casts of characters, there were revisions in both "Was" and "The Old People" that reflected the racial concerns of "The Bear." Originally Faulkner had not put any particular stress on Sam Fathers's being a mulatto; but in working out the later version of "The Bear" he had seen that Sam's mixed blood could be used to relate the hunting episodes to Isaac McCaslin's discovery of racial evil in the fourth section. He had made Sam's having had to endure being a black all of his seventy years the explanation of his acceptance of Lion, whose appearance foretold the fated death of Old Ben. And he had had Sam, when he finally reached his small dark hut after the hunt was over and the bear was dead, say to Major de Spain, "Let me out, master . . . . Let me go home."

When he returned to "The Old People," Faulkner transformed Sam's "slave woman" mother into a quadroon and added an explanation of his feelings about his mixed inheritance. When Isaac noticed an odd expression that sometimes appeared in Sam's eyes when they were in repose, his cousin McCaslin explained to him that every now and then the old man smelled the cage of his bondage. "Let him go" was the boy's immediate response, but his older cousin understood that physical liberation would not change things. He remarked that Sam's cage was not the McCaslins but himself, that in all probability he did not resent his chieftain father's selling him into slavery but felt betrayed by his mother "who had bequeathed him not only the blood of slaves but even a little of the very blood which had enslaved it."[2] He was "himself his own

battleground, the scene of his own vanquishment and the mauso-
leum of his defeat."

In "Was" a slight but significant change was made in the role
played by Tomey's Turl. At first Faulkner had conceived him as
simply a worthless slave, somewhat like Percival Brownlee, whom
Uncle Buck could not sell in Memphis because his reputation for
incompetence had already reached into Tennessee. On a discarded
page from an early typescript, Uncle Buck said that he had once considered sending him "under government frank to President Buchanan
as a present except that he couldn't unload Tomey's Turl even on
somebody he thought as little of as he done President Buchanan."[3]
In the typescript in the Alderman Library, Turl was no longer
described as generally worthless. He remained a nuisance only in
his continual running away to visit Tennie, but he was still pictured
as wholly Negro and dark in color. Great emphasis was placed on
the blackness of his arms as he dealt fateful poker hands.

In the final version he is referred to by Hubert Beauchamp as
"that damn white half-McCaslin," and at the crucial moment in
Turl's dealing the poker hands to Mr. Hubert Beauchamp and Uncle
Buddy, young Cass Edmonds becomes aware that his arms "that
were supposed to be black . . . were not quite white." This change
was made just before the final typescript of the book was sent to the
printer. It provides the most important of Faulkner's suggestions to
his readers that there were grimmer aspects of slaveholding southern
society than were apparent to the nine-year-old boy through whose
view the story was told. Hints of unpleasant complexities beneath
the delightful comic surface of this introductory story of *Go Down,
Moses* prepare the way for the darker revelations of the fourth section of "The Bear," discovered by a sixteen-year-old who could not
resist exploring yellowed ledgers to learn what his family's past
really was.

CHAPTER EIGHT

"THE FIRE AND THE HEARTH"

FAULKNER'S MOST IMPORTANT revisions were made in the first and last of the three stories included in "The Fire and the Hearth," and in "Delta Autumn." These were primarily changes in characterization rather than in plot. In revised form the stories comprising "The Fire and the Hearth" are still concerned with the discovery of hidden whiskey stills, with the quest for buried treasure, and with the calling off of tragicomic divorce proceedings.

And in the rewritten portions of these stories the apparently comic, patronizing treatment of blacks established in the opening story of the book, "Was," which took place on the eve of the Civil War, was carried down to the present in Faulkner's fictional Mississippi of 1940 or 1941. But once he had made Lucas's landlord, Carothers Edmonds, a relative of the McCaslin family and had made Lucas himself a McCaslin, the oldest still living on the ancestral land, Faulkner saw the need of drawing his major figures in deeper chiaroscura. As a result he interpolated passages, particularly two extended accounts of interracial crises recalled in memory by Lucas and by Roth, which shatter the comfortable tone which had char-

acterized the narration of the original stories and which jolt his
reader out of any complacency he may feel toward black and white
relationships in Go Down, Moses. The interpolations serve to suggest that Faulkner's apparent complacency about slavery in "Was"
was only apparent, and they serve to prepare the reader for the
shocks which lie ahead of him when he reads on past more apparent
complacency toward slavery into the heart of the labyrinth of
McCaslin family history which lies in the ledgers in the fourth part
of "The Bear."

In addition to these interpolations which make his portrayal of
Roth and Lucas more forceful and more complex, Faulkner inserted
a variety of shorter passages referring to Old Carothers McCaslin,
to McCaslin Edmonds, and to his major protagonist, who is now, by
the time these stories take place about 1940, Uncle Ike McCaslin.
These passages—besides the material added to "The Fire and the
Hearth" there are three paragraphs placed at the opening of the
book to serve as a general introduction to Go Down, Moses—anticipate the fourth section of "The Bear" and might seem intended to
prepare us for that notably complex piece of writing. But these
interpolations are not especially helpful as preparatory explanations.
Complicated references to characters not yet introduced into the
plot are in themselves confusing. And by the time anyone has made
his way to "The Bear," he has pretty well forgotten the information
that has been disclosed about its major white personalities in the
passages added to the earlier stories. Many of these passages are in
themselves incomprehensible when they are first read, long before
a reader has any sense of what the fourth section is about. What
can the reader who has not yet learned anything concerning Isaac's
grandfather make of Lucas's saying to Zack Edmonds, "I got to
beat old Carothers. Get your pistol,"[1] and, on the other hand, thinking to himself, "So I reckon I aint got old Carothers' blood for
nothing, after all. Old Carothers, . . . I needed him and he come
and spoke for me?"[2] What can a reader make of the references to
Isaac, who is presented in one place as a man aware that he "re-
neged, cried calf-rope, sold . . . [his] birthright, betrayed . . . [his]
blood, for . . . obliteration, and a little food,"[3] and a few pages
earlier as a secular saint who had been born old but who "became
steadily younger and younger until, past seventy . . . he had ac-

quired something of a young boy's high and selfless innocence."[4]

The contradictions between passages like these stem in part
from Faulkner's own ambivalence. As a southerner and as a Falkner
—christened William Cuthbert Falkner II after his great-grandfather
—he was unable to see Isaac McCaslin's action in turning away from
his grandfather and renouncing his family heritage as simply as
liberal northerners often have. Many of his later remarks about Isaac
seem to reflect a deep inner uncertainty as to whether he admired
Isaac's moral gesture of repudiation or considered it evidence of
insufficient humanity. In September 1955 he questioned Cynthia
Grenier's choosing Isaac as her favorite Faulkner character, re-
marking that "a man ought to do more than just repudiate. He
should have been more affirmative instead of shunning people."[5] He
later compared Isaac's conduct to those who reject what is rotten
in society and "go off into a cave or climb a pillar to sit on" instead
of saying "this is bad and I'm going to do something about it, I'm
going to change it."[6] But at another time Faulkner had affirmed that
Isaac had been true to the teachings of Sam Fathers, had fulfilled
his moral destiny, and had gained, instead of success, serenity and
"what would pass for wisdom . . . contradistinct from the school-
man's wisdom of education."[7]

Another source of contradictions in the passages added to the
earlier stories was Faulkner's method of revision. It seems safe to
assume that he began revising these stories only after he had completed his revision of "The Bear." But Faulkner was a constant
tinkerer (recall the last-minute changes in "Was"), and he found
portions of the revised version of "The Bear" unsatisfactory after he
rewrote the other stories. Almost nothing remains of the earlier
drafts of the final version of "The Bear,"[8] but evidence of Faulkner's
process of revision can be found in several discrepancies in the final
text of *Go Down, Moses*. Several are apparent if the account of the
early years of Tennie Beauchamp's children, which was added to
the typescript story "The Fire and the Hearth,"[9] is compared to that
in the fourth section of "The Bear." In the account in "The Fire and
the Hearth" James is described as having simply run away "before
he became of age," but in "The Bear" his departure is placed precisely on the "*night of his twenty-first birthday Dec 29 1885*," and
mention is made of his cousin Isaac's efforts to locate him.[10] In "The

Fire and the Hearth" Faulkner made Isaac's mother the teacher of Lucas, Jim, and Fonsiba, and each child inherited one-third of "a sum of money, with the accumulated interest" provided by their white half-uncles, Buck and Buddy. Isaac McCaslin received fifty dollars each month from his cousin for the farm he had renounced, and he accompanied Fonsiba and her husband to Arkansas after their wedding, transferred her third of the legacy to a local bank, and arranged for her to draw three dollars each week. In "The Bear" it is McCaslin Edmonds's wife Alice who taught Fonsiba to read and write, and the inheritances of the children are based upon Carothers McCaslin's thousand-dollar bequest to his son Terrel, their father, and have been increased by Buck and Buddy to a thousand dollars for each child.[11] In "The Bear" Isaac accepted only thirty dollars a month from McCaslin Edmonds and that as a loan which he repaid, and the financial arrangements with the Arkansas bank, which ensued from Isaac's epic journey to locate the newly married couple, provided Fonsiba with three dollars a month instead of three dollars a week.[12] When these discrepancies are compared, it becomes reasonably certain that the versions in "The Bear" are the later ones. Isaac's mother's death is placed in "The Bear" at about his tenth birthday,[13] so it would have been difficult for her to have taught much of anything to Lucas Beauchamp, who was born in 1874, seven years after her son. The accounts of the augmented legacies and of the financial arrangements made between Isaac and Fonsiba and between Isaac and his cousin, McCaslin, are more carefully and more elaborately worked out in "The Bear" than in "The Fire and the Hearth" and seem to have been added to the text of the fourth section after Faulkner's original expansion and revision of the story.

The discrepancies in details stemming from Faulkner's ambivalent feelings, from his carelessness, and from his restless need to develop more intricately imagined accounts of the lives of his characters each time he returned to them are of no great importance. They are probably unnoticed by most readers. But the shifting and seemingly contradictory attitudes shown by Lucas Beauchamp and by Roth Edmonds toward Isaac McCaslin and his grandfather, old Carothers, are significant; they add considerably to the complexity of Faulkner's characterization of the two men. Their full importance

becomes apparent only after many readings. It is difficult to deter-
mine whether this is due primarily to carelessness or to design.
Faulkner's contempt for the lazy reader, his insistence that his books
be read as many times as are necessary to disclose his meaning, a
fourth time if three have not been sufficient, is well known.[14] He may
have counted on securing his effects by forcing his readers to make
several readings, as he had in the great experimental novels written
between 1929 and 1936. It is certainly true that these passages are
fully effective only when they are read as they were written, after
"The Bear."[15] Yet few readers will ever give a work as uneven as
Go Down, Moses more than one reading. Little complaint can be
made of the heavy demands which Faulkner makes of readers of
The Sound and the Fury and Absalom, Absalom!, but an expectation
of several readings seems ill founded in a work built with pieces of
very noticeably uneven weight and formed only partially into an
organic whole, a work still bearing marks of its piecemeal composition, filled with discrepancies of detail. It is not surprising that most
of Faulkner's readers have concentrated on the major part of this
work, "The Bear," and have pretty consistently ignored the incom-
pletely unified whole.

However understandable the concentration upon "The Bear"
and, to a lesser extent, upon "Was" and "Delta Autumn," it is re-
warding to examine Faulkner's efforts to unify the volume. Take the
changes he made in Carothers Edmonds. As originally conceived in
the comic stories about gold hunting and moonshining, Roth seemed
a fairly typical well-to-do southern white man, skeptically tolerant
of the vagaries of blacks. Yet even in the early versions of the stories
he revealed qualities unrelated to the conventional role he had to
play. He was capable of surprising sensitivity and diffidence in
gazing out of his car window at the masklike face of Lucas Beauchamp and thinking to himself that Lucas came from a race which
was pure many thousand years before his own became mixed enough
to produce a man like himself.[16] In the process of rewriting the three
stories that formed the basis of the individual chapters of "The Fire
and the Hearth" so that they would fit more gracefully both genea-
logically and thematically into a volume organized around his revised version of "The Bear," Faulkner had gradually added to Roth's
age and had increased the intimacy of Roth's relationship to Molly

Beauchamp until it resembled his own relationship to Callie Barr.
The revisions Faulkner made in his characterization of Roth
after he conceived the fourth section of "The Bear" might be regarded as an effort to realize fully a phrase he had used quite
casually in the second typescript of the third chapter of "The Fire
and the Hearth," describing Roth's sense of Lucas as an old man
"who had emerged out of the tragic complexity of his motherless
childhood as the husband of the woman who had been the only
mother he knew." Faulkner added a passage describing regular
monthly visits Roth paid to Molly's house—much like visits he himself paid to Callie's—with small bags of candy and tins of tobacco
for her clay pipe. These visits, he wrote, were thought of by
Edmonds as libations to his luck, but they were in reality libations
"to his ancestors and to the conscience which he would have probably affirmed he did not possess, in the form, the person, of the
negro woman"[17] whom he had known as his only mother.

But in addition to making Roth more sympathetic by giving a
fuller account of his connection with Molly and Lucas Beauchamp
—giving Roth something of his own sensitivity to racial relationships, Faulkner also made him explicitly the heir of his ruthless
ancestor, Carothers McCaslin, rechanging his name to Carothers
Edmonds after it had been converted to McCaslin Edmonds, just
before the final typescript went off to the printer.[18] He also put him
in "Delta Autumn" in the role of the cynical lover whom he had
originally named Don Boyd.[19]

It was difficult to amalgamate in a single character both his
own sympathetic concern for blacks and the destructive cynicism of
Don Boyd. Faulkner never managed to disguise fully the discrepancy
between the Roth Edmonds of the third chapter of "The Fire and
the Hearth" and the Roth Edmonds of the final version of "Delta
Autumn." To achieve wholly credible consistency, he would have
had to make the characterization of Edmonds in "Delta Autumn"
much more subtle. For the Roth Edmonds of the Lucas Beauchamp
stories is a convincingly complicated human being, and his feelings
about blacks are especially complex. In these stories his reactions
range very nearly from those of a Don Boyd to those of a William
Faulkner

The most arresting of the passages Faulkner wrote to fill out his characterization of Roth is the description of a fall from grace at the age of seven.[20] Roth's life before his lapse into inherited racial evil had been a domestic idyll comparable to young Isaac McCaslin's pastoral existence before the appearance of Lion. For his first seven years Roth had lived in two interchangeable households, free of racial consciousness, accepting Lucas as fully as he accepted his own father and centering his affection on one woman, who was black. He and his foster brother, Henry, ate at the same tables and slept on the same pallet or bed. They lived in simple innocence around the night time hearth with its fire burning even in summer, and during the days they were off in the fields with hounds for hunting and with a promise of guns when they got a trifle older. "They were sufficient, complete, wanting as all children do, not to be understood . . . but only to love, to question . . . and to be let alone." But one night the serpent of ancestral pride, the old curse of his white fathers, descended to Roth and, lying rigid in shame and grief which he could neither understand nor admit, he turned Henry away from his bed, which they had shared.

Few things in "The Bear" are more powerful than Faulkner's account of Roth's growing realization of the magnitude of what he had done, of his avoidance of Molly's house for a month, and his recognition—once he was ready to admit his grief and shame—that it was too late. He walked over to Molly's and announced that he would eat with them all that night. Molly promised him a chicken for supper. But when he was called into the house after he had watched Henry do his milking in the barn and whiled away the time in the yard, he missed Lucas and saw that "there was just one chair, one plate, his glass of milk beside it" and that Henry was about to go out of the door. In this way Roth "entered his heritage. He ate its bitter fruit."

Part of that bitter heritage was having to put up with Lucas, having to observe him deliberately avoid calling his father Mister Zack or directly by any other name at all. Once he asked his father why he put up with Lucas's behavior and was irritated rather than satisfied by his father's explaining that he and Lucas had eaten and slept, hunted and fished together until they were grown men. He felt that there was something more between the white man and the black one and later he sensed that it was over a woman—a black woman. Outraged by the suspicion that Lucas had somehow bested his father over a black woman—he never once thought of Molly—he felt bitterly contemptuous of the whole Edmonds line. *"Edmonds. Even a nigger McCaslin is a better man, better than all of us. Old Carothers got his nigger bastards right in his backyard and I would like to have seen the husband or anybody else that said him nay."*

But if Roth could be exasperated by Lucas into an admiration of the callous old days when nothing inhibited white men from being men enough to get their nigger bastards right in their own backyards, he also saw Lucas himself as a recognizable throwback to their common progenitor. Faulkner describes him, after he had succeeded his father as master of the McCaslin place, sitting at his lonely bachelor supper which he could not eat, musing about Lucas's behavior and picturing his face once again before him, seeing it as "a composite of a whole generation of fierce and undefeated young Confederate soldiers."[21] Roth then thought with shock and something approaching horror,

"He's more like old Carothers than all the rest of us put together. . . . He is both heir and prototype simultaneously of all the geography and climate and biology which sired old Carothers and all the rest of us and our kind, myriad, countless, faceless, even nameless now except himself who fathered himself, intact and complete, contemptuous, as old Carothers must have been, of all blood black white yellow or red, including his own."

Roth Edmonds's instinctive turning back to old Carothers McCaslin when confronted by the intransigence of Lucas is surprising, but Lucas's own preoccupation with the old man is startling. When Faulkner transformed Lucas from a sharecropper into the oldest McCaslin still in possession of family land, he made him much more self-conscious, and one of the things Lucas is most conscious of is his white ancestor, his grandfather and the oppressor of his race, who had died thirty-seven years before he was born.

The revised portions of the first chapter of "The Fire and the Hearth," those most revealing of Lucas's states of mind as those of the third chapter are of Roth's, begin with Lucas groping in total darkness through a creek bottom, seeking a hiding place for his still so that he could safely expose the whiskey manufacturing of his prospective son-in-law, George Wilkins. He settled on a nearly sym-

metrical flat-topped Indian mound and started digging under an
overhang on one side, to save himself a little work. Just when the
opening was big enough, the whole overhang toppled, avalanching
in the dark over the hollow kettle and the worm and spilling over
Lucas, too, until a final something larger than a clod caught him
solidly in the face, "a blow not vicious so much as merely heavy-
handed, a sort of final admonitory pat from the spirit of darkness
and solitude, the old earth, perhaps the old ancestors themselves."
The things that struck him turned out to be a piece of a large pottery
jug, which crumbled away as he picked it up, leaving in his hand
the single gold coin that provoked him into the foolishness of treasure hunting. His first thought was to take George Wilkins in as a
minor partner in gold-seeking so that he could have help with the
digging and also in order to render "a sort of justice, balance, liba-
tion to chance and fortune" because George had been indirectly
responsible for his finding the coin. But Faulkner makes him reject
the idea almost immediately out of pride in his sense of himself as
a McCaslin. "He, Lucas Beauchamp, the oldest living McCaslin
descendant still living on the hereditary land, who actually remembered old Buck and Buddy in the living flesh[22] . . . he, to share one
jot, one penny of the money which [he thought] old Buck and
Buddy had buried almost a hundred years ago, with an interloper
without forbears and sprung from nowhere and whose very name
was unknown in the country twenty-five years ago."

Not only is Lucas conscious of his being a McCaslin, he is ex-
tremely aware of his role as the last of an older generation. He is
scornful of Roth, who seems to him less of a man than his father,
Zack; and he likes to think of himself as kindred in spirit to Roth's
grandfather, old Cass Edmonds. Lucas's family pride and his sense
of forceful maleness not only lead him to identify himself with
members of the family notable for their ruthlessness, but also be-
guile him into contemptuousness of Isaac McCaslin. He is misled
into admiring what he regarded—without understanding the issues
at stake—as McCaslin Edmonds's ruthlessness in gaining possession
of the family land from the rightful heir. He even goes so far as to
look back approvingly on Cass as having been "old Carothers
McCaslin enough" to get what he wanted.

The most interesting aspects of Lucas's ambivalent fascination with his white grandfather are revealed in the extended passage describing Lucas's recollections of his altercation with Zack over Molly shortly after Roth's birth, a passage which Faulkner added to the first chapter.[23] There, as in Lucas's present deluded search for buried gold, a compelling concern with his white ancestor is linked to his self-regard and to his foolishness. At the time when Roth was born, Lucas had, out of loyalty to Zack and to the memory of old Carothers, risked his life in the boiling, timber-choked creek to go for a doctor only to find on his return that the mother was dead and Molly was ensconced as nurse and cook in the white man's house with her recently born son, Henry. After putting up with the situation for nearly six months, Lucas went to Zack's and demanded his wife, muttering, almost despite himself, "I reckon you thought I wouldn't take her back, didn't you?" When he returned home after finishing the day's plowing, he found Molly settled in with the two babies. Infuriated because she did not sense that he suspected her of carrying on with Zack, Lucas refused to believe her when she said that the white man had agreed to her taking his son back to her home. He spent the evening waiting for Zack to come over to ask for his child back, thinking, *He will do something and then I will do something and it will be all over. It will be all right.*

But it was not all right. Zack put out the light in his house which Lucas had been watching and, instead of crossing over to Lucas's, went quietly to bed. Considering Zack's conduct contemptuous of his manhood, Lucas waited for daylight and was standing razor in hand over the white man's bed when his eyes opened. "You knowed I wasn't afraid," Lucas tells Zack, "because you knowed I was a McCaslin too and a man-made one." But "you thought that because I am a nigger I wouldn't even mind. I never figured on the razor neither. But I gave you your chance. Maybe I didn't know what I might have done when you walked in my door, but I knowed what I wanted to do, what I believed I was going to do, what Carothers McCaslin would have wanted me to do."

A little later, after the bright blade has been flung out the open window, Lucas's white ancestor has been transformed from a psychological support into an inhibiting force. Lucas tells Zack to get his pistol: "All you got to beat is me. I got to beat old Carothers." A moment later he says, "I done already beat you. . . . It's old

Carothers. Get your pistol, white man." Zack understands after he
has tossed his pistol on the bed and challenged Lucas to an Indian-
wrestling match for it that he has pushed him too far, to a point from
which he cannot back down. Lucas's eyes redden like those of a
bayed animal, and he forces the white arm down. Suddenly he has
the pistol, and he tells Zack, "You thought I wouldn't, didn't you. . . .
You knowed I could beat you, so you thought to beat me with old
Carothers, like Cass Edmonds done Isaac," expounding the very
curious notion that McCaslin Edmonds in the scene in the commissary described in the fourth section of "The Bear" was able to
use the memory of the original McCaslin to get the better of his
cousin because he was "the woman-made McCaslin, the woman
branch, the sister." According to Lucas's remarkably odd reasoning,
Ike knew that his grandfather would have wanted him to "give in to
woman-kin that couldn't fend for herself." And, Lucas tells Zack,

You thought I'd do that too, didn't you? You thought I'd do it quick, quicker
than Isaac since it aint any land I would give up . . . . All I got to give up is
McCaslin blood that rightfully aint even mine or at least aint worth much since
old Carothers never seemed to miss much what he give to Tomey that night
that made my father. And if this is what that McCaslin blood has brought me,
I dont want it neither.

In a last desperate effort to vindicate his manhood and recapture
his sense of himself as a McCaslin before he pulls the trigger for the
shot that misfires, Lucas shouts,

Say I don't even use this first bullet at all [If he used two bullets the second
would be for himself], say I just uses this last one and beat you and old
Carothers both, leave you something to think about now and then when you
aint too busy to try to think up what to tell old Carothers when you get where
he's done already gone, tomorrow and the one after that and the one after that
as long as tomorrow.

Later, trudging along behind his plow through the rows of
vigorous half-grown corn in that year of the long summer, Lucas
examined carefully the cartridge which had not fired. It was hardly
as large as his little finger yet big enough to have held two lives
because, as he thought with satisfaction, "*I wouldn't have used the
second one. . . . I would have paid* [by allowing himself to be
lynched]. *So I reckon I aint got old Carothers' blood for nothing,*

after all. Old Carothers, . . . I needed him and he come and spoke for me." In the end the thought of his white grandfather has again become a comfort for Lucas, a sustenance to his manhood. But his suspicion of Molly remains unresolved even though the reader has little doubt that she is innocent.[24] Lucas concludes that he would prefer staying uncertain to discovering later that he had been deceived. And the episode ends with his plaint, "How to God . . . can a black man ask a white man to please not lay down with his black wife? And even if he could ask it, how to God can the white man promise he wont?"

Among the more striking of Faulkner's additions to the text of "The Fire and the Hearth" are a series of references to the character and actions of Isaac McCaslin.[25] At least one is in Faulkner's own narrative voice, and others are attributed to the thoughts of Lucas Beauchamp and to those of Isaac himself. The image of the man that emerges from these additions is curiously blurred. They are confusing and seem to reflect confusion. Faulkner's ambivalent feelings about Isaac are made a part of Lucas's consciousness. His varying attitudes toward Ike parallel his uncertainty about that very different white man, the common grandfather, Carothers McCaslin. While he wandered at night through the tangled creek bottom searching for a hiding place for his whiskey-making apparatus, Lucas thought of Isaac as a kinsman unjustly cheated out of his patrimony;[26] and a few moments later, after he failed to discover more than the single gold coin in the toppled Indian mound, he saw him as an apostate to his lineage, who had weakly renounced land that was rightfully his.[27] The most curious of Lucas's musings about Isaac occurred a few pages farther on in the story in the passage in which he recalled his struggle with Zack over Molly. Lucas then considered Isaac the hapless victim of his older cousin's shrewdness in invoking Carothers McCaslin's gallant concern for womankind in order to deprive the younger man of his landed inheritance.

CHAPTER NINE

"DELTA AUTUMN"

MUCH MORE IMPORTANT than these references to Isaac McCaslin which Faulkner added to the stories about Lucas Beauchamp are the revisions he made when he returned to "Delta Autumn" after having described the youth and young manhood of its aged protagonist in "The Bear."[1] The original narrative, published in *Story* magazine, had presented a melancholy old man who had endured beyond his time into an alien America of shrunken woods, lingering depression, and impending war. Old Isaac's habitual hopefulness had served only to make him more pitiable.

A substantial modification of the old man's character might have seemed in order when Faulkner came back to the story after having created the scene of the young Isaac's measured acceptance of good and evil, of life and of death, in saluting the mysterious serpent as "chief" and "grandfather." But the changes Faulkner made in the story stem from no readily apparent alteration in his conception of the old man; they seem to reflect his own uncertainty about young Isaac's act of renunciation. Just as Faulkner made Lucas Beauchamp no wiser in transforming him into a McCaslin, actually making him foolish in the McCaslin pretentiousness of his admiration for old Carothers, so he bestowed on the old hunter little of the serene wisdom he had won as a young man in "The Bear."

Perhaps because of discouraging limitations apparent in Old Isaac in "Delta Autumn," Faulkner at one time planned to place that story before "The Bear" in *Go Down, Moses*.[2] Such an order would have left the reader with a relatively hopeful view of the career of Isaac McCaslin. In the present order "Delta Autumn" serves to reinforce an episode Faulkner conceived as early as 1935 for "Lion," the first of his stories of the hunt for Old Ben. The concluding scene of "The Bear," the image of frenzied idiocy presented by Boon Hogganbeck hammering his gun barrel against the breech in a futile effort to get at the treeful of swirling squirrels he madly claimed as his, is immediately followed by the opening paragraphs of "Delta Autumn." This arrangement causes the tone of nostalgia pervading these paragraphs to arise directly from the glimpse of Boon's imbecilic futility at the end of "The Bear."

All of "Delta Autumn" gains power from its placing in *Go Down, Moses* as an epilogue to the epic events of Isaac McCaslin's youth. Phrases which could have had only casual importance to readers of the May-June issue of *Story* magazine have a different significance for readers of *Go Down, Moses*.

> Soon now they would enter the Delta. The sensation was familiar to him. It had been renewed like this each last week in November for more than fifty years. . . .
> At first they had come in wagons. . . . There had been bear then. . . . But that time was gone now. Now they went in cars . . . the territory in which game still existed drawing yearly inward as his life was drawing inward, until now he was the last of those who had once made the journey in wagons . . . . They called him "Uncle Ike" now.

Faulkner did not modify his method of narration significantly. The point of view is still focused primarily within the consciousness of the old hunter. But he did carefully revise the two interludes of dramatic conversation during which the point of view had shifted away from the old man's mind so that the reader saw him from the outside, more objectively, in what was often argumentative discussion. And Faulkner's first important addition to the text was a scene at the dinner table under newly erected, rain-swept canvas. This

scene, which occupies five pages of *Go Down, Moses*, presents the
aged Isaac McCaslin's oracular discourse concerning hunting and
love, the nature of man, and the nature of God and his ultimate
retribution. Isaac's rambling monologue is so inconsistent that if it
were not reminiscent of portions of the argument in the fourth section of "The Bear," it would appear that Faulkner must be treating
the old man ironically.

The discourse begins in great optimism, concludes in bleak
pessimism, and is interrupted by the younger men's joking about
Roth Edmonds's luck in "doe" hunting, which Isaac seems only partially to understand. At the start he proclaims his belief in human
goodness, his belief that most men are at all times "a little better
than their circumstances give them a chance to be." And, he continues, the world was created by God as a paradise on earth for
man, "the kind of world He would have wanted to live in if He had
been a man—the ground to walk on, the big woods, the trees and the
water, and the game to live in it." Even the desire to kill game, if
not created in man by God, was foreknown and tolerated by Him
because man "wasn't quite God himself yet." Asked by one of his
listeners when man will get to be God, old Isaac goes on to declare
that every man and woman, at the instant of love for each other
when it becomes irrelevant "whether they marry then or afterward
or dont never," are together God. At this point Roth mutters, "Then
there are some Gods in this world I wouldn't want to touch . . . with
a damn long stick. . . . And that includes myself," and he heads off
for bed.

After the departure of Roth, Faulkner picks out three black
faces in the audience, "dark and motionless and musing." And when
the old man resumes his speculations concerning God's foreknowledge of man's desire to hunt and kill, his former hopefulness has
evaporated. Somberness anticipatory of the conclusion of the story
colors his discourse as it comes to an end. "I believe He said, 'So be
it.' I reckon He even foreknew the end. But He said, 'I will give
him his chance. I will give him warning and foreknowledge too. . . .
The woods and fields he ravages and the game he devastates will be
the consequence and signature of his crime and guilt, and his punish-
ment.' "[3]

Faulkner's next important additions to the text recall episodes of Isaac's life presented earlier in *Go Down, Moses* and reinterpret them. In the original version of "Delta Autumn" Ike had remembered his old companions on the hunt and, particularly, Sam Fathers's ritual action of marking his face with blood when he had killed his first buck. In revising the story Faulkner explicitly linked Sam's baptism in the woods with the scene in the commissary at the time of Ike's coming of age, which he had presented at length in the fourth section of "The Bear." Faulkner related the boy's general resolution to make his life worthy of the buck he had slain to his particular act of repudiating his inheritance from Carothers Mc-Caslin. In "The Bear" Isaac's long-winded arguments had seemed frequently naïve and sometimes fatuous, distorted by self-concern. McCaslin Edmonds had had a more honest and realistic conception of a person's relationship to all he had inherited from his family and his culture. In re-presenting that discussion as it was remembered by the old man, Faulkner subtly altered it. He did not attempt to make the youthful Ike seem greatly wiser, but he did make him more modest in his aims and, therefore, more likable. He described him as one who had tried to repudiate the tainted land and the shame and the wrong, as one who in his boyhood had believed he could both cure the wrong and remove the shame but who

at twenty-one . . . knew that he could do neither[4] but at least he could re-pudiate the wrong and shame, at least in principle, and at least the land itself in fact, for his son at least: and did, thought he had: then (married then) in a rented cubicle in a back-street stock-traders' boarding-house, . . . himself and his wife juxtaposed in their turn against that same land, that same wrong and shame from whose regret and grief he would at least save and free his son and, saving and freeing his son, lost him.

The young Isaac has become a more sympathetic figure in retro-spect because his hopes have been made more limited and because his defeat, implicit in the grotesque scene of his wife's attempted sexual blackmail which concluded the fourth part of "The Bear," has been made explicit. And Faulkner's sympathetic reinterpretation extends even to the wife whom Ike had regarded in "The Bear" as evidence of universal human depravity, proof that "we were all born lost." In "Delta Autumn" Ike's loss of his wife is ascribed not to her desire for the farm he had inherited, as "The Bear" had suggested, but to her unlimited love for him.[5] And Faulkner's emphasis in "The Bear" on the jaded sexual sophistication of women, "born already bored with what a boy approaches . . . with blundering and aghast trembling," is replaced by an admiring account of feminine capacity for hope and love.

These reinterpretations of episodes in "The Bear" suggest a softening in Faulkner, a mellowing of his sense of human aspirations and human defeats. This mellowing is in accord with the opening hopeful portion of old Isaac's discourse over the dinner table, and it may represent the most characteristic view of mankind presented by Faulkner in this story and in *Go Down, Moses* as a whole. It is, however, in jarring contradiction to the despairing pessimism with which the old man had concluded his pronouncement at the table, and also to the melancholy lament for the delta "deswamped and denuded and derivered [by man] in two generations" which Faulkner retained at the end of the story from the magazine version.

Most important of all the changes Faulkner made in revising "Delta Autumn" were those concerning the scene between old Isaac and the mulatto girl who had borne Don Boyd's child. Originally, when the young woman invaded the canvas-walled sanctuary in which the old hunter had just come drowsily awake and received from him an envelope of smooth, neat bills left behind by her lover, Boyd's callousness seemed, in itself, as central to the story as the reaction it produced in the old man. Isaac McCaslin's role appeared to be primarily that of a witness to the type of behavior that had led to the ravishment of the wilderness rather than that of an actor in his own right. His presenting Boyd's money to the unknown woman in no way disqualified him from serving as judge of Boyd's conduct. He stood safely apart from it, dismayed but uninvolved.

Faulkner changed this in the revised version by substituting Roth Edmonds for Don Boyd. As a result, Isaac McCaslin, who had once renounced his inheritance to avoid its stain, is trapped in the middle of an unhappy affair between two members of his own family, passing money from the white to the black. His involvement is underlined by the young woman's accusing him of spoiling Roth "when [he] gave to [Roth's] grandfather that land which didn't belong to him."

In the earlier version of the story, she had seemed more alert and perceptive than the old man, and Faulkner heightened this impression in his revisions. He added a passage describing Isaac's fumbling with the envelope of bills to contrast with the description of the girl's neat precision in opening it. More important, he has her, almost at the start, declare to the uncomprehending old man, "You're Uncle Isaac," and comment with knowing irony upon the "honor" involved in Roth's telling her "what his code I suppose he would call it would forbid him forever to do."

Originally old Ike had asked the young woman what she really wanted from Boyd, and she had replied quietly, apparently pointlessly, "Yes." In revision Faulkner added to McCaslin's question another, more significant one, "What do you expect?" and he no longer left the girl's "yes" dangling without immediate significance. He added in explanation of it her tracing Roth's lineage back to the original McCaslin, the sire of both branches of the family, "His . . . great great *great* grandfather was your grandfather. McCaslin. Only it got to be Edmonds." What could one expect from such an inheritance? As she proceeded, she continued to use the ambiguous pronoun "it," referring to the family name and to much more. "Only it got to be more than that. Your cousin McCaslin was there that day when your father and Uncle Buddy won Tennie from Mr. Beauchamp for the one that had no name but Terrel so you called him Tomey's Terrel, to marry. But after that it got to be Edmonds."

Old Isaac can make nothing of this. He asks no questions. He has not emerged from his drowsy lethargy enough to wonder how she learned so much about his family. He can only reply stupidly, "Me? . . . Me?" when she accuses him of bearing the greatest share of the responsibility for Roth's having become the man he is.

A passage, amplified during Faulkner's revision of the story, that expressed the old man's generous but obtuse concern for an educated woman who could allow herself to be used and discarded by a man she met casually in the street concluded in a sentence which had no particular importance originally but which took on immense ironic force in the new context. "Haven't you got any folks at all?" The full significance of the woman's reply, her second enigmatic "yes," is not apparent to McCaslin. Only after she goes on to identify "one of them," an aunt who took in washing in Vicksburg, does the old man rise from his torpor and blurt, "You're a nigger!" This outburst and her quiet reply, her third and ultimate "yes," were included in the original version. But at this point Faulkner added a passage greatly altering and intensifying their meaning. Surely one of the most dramatic moments in *Go Down, Moses* is here, in her placid reply to the old man's outraged and dismayed accusation that she is a nigger. " 'Yes,' she said. 'James Beauchamp—you called him Tennie's Jim though he had a name—was my grandfather. I said you were Uncle Isaac.' "

That she is a nigger and that he is nevertheless her Uncle Isaac is too overwhelming for the old man to acknowledge, for him to respond to directly. Instead he shifts her attention from himself to her association with his relative, asking her whether Roth knew the identity of her grandfather. Despite his very substantial alteration in Isaac McCaslin's relationship to the young woman, Faulkner retained the passage in which the old hunter ordered her away and insisted that she take Roth's money out of his tent, as though he could thereby avoid being contaminated with it and with the sorry love affair. In this the old man resembles the young man who had attempted to renounce his tainted heritage in the fourth section of "The Bear." But ultimately the significance of what she has said penetrates his aged mind, and he does acknowledge that he is indeed "Uncle Isaac." He reaches out his light, dry old man's fingers and touches the "smooth young flesh [of her hand] where the strong old blood ran after its long lost journey back to home" and repeats her words, "Tennie's Jim. . . . Tennie's Jim." Possibly smarting under her careful emphasis upon white McCaslin practices in naming black McCaslins, her reference to "the one that had no name but Terrel so you called him Tomey's Terrel" (concerning whom he himself had years before thought bitterly of his grandfather's legacy to his black relatives, *"I reckon that was cheaper than saying My son to a nigger"*) and her reference to "James Beauchamp—you called him Tennie's Jim though he had a name," Isaac cannot hold back one final bitter remark about Terrel's mother, which echoes the phrasing of the young woman's description of the son. He says of the blanket-wrapped infant she holds, "It's a boy, I reckon. They usually are, except the one that was its own mother too." Despite this unsuppressible, if momentary, brutality, Isaac, now more than seventy years old, realizes that at long last he has found the end of the trail of Tennie's Jim, which he had lost in Jackson, Tennessee, almost a lifetime before, when he was eighteen. Then he had assumed the family burden and attempted to force on Jim his share of the legacy left to the black descendants whom Carothers McCaslin had been incapable of acknowledging publicly. Now instead of money he gives something more precious to him, a thing symbolic of the heroic age of the big woods. On the infant great-grandson of "Tennie's Jim," his cousin and ubiquitous hunting companion who had been with him when Sam Fathers had died, he bestows the horn willed him by old General Compson.

Symbolically, the old man's gesture is immense; practically, it is empty. What can it mean to the youngest of old Carothers's descendants? What can it do to alter his life? Yet it is all that Isaac McCaslin, limited by his age, his culture, and the way he has chosen to live his life, has to give. His subsequent remarks, wisely retained by Faulkner without substantial change from the *Story* version, seem, in this altered context, to reflect an old man's bitter sense of impotence. He urges his cousin, Carothers Edmonds's mistress, to go North, to marry a man of her "own race. That's the only salvation . . . for a while yet, maybe a long while yet."[6] His offering her cynical advice about finding a black husband who would value her handsome white skin provokes her devastating question as to whether he had "lived so long and forgotten so much" that he could no longer remember anything he had once known about love.

It was relatively easy for a boy of eighteen in the summery woods of "The Bear" to acknowledge the existence of evil symbolically by greeting an aged snake as "grandfather." It is beyond possibility for an old white man to be of any practical help to his black relatives in the shrunken autumnal wilderness of this story. In "Delta Autumn" the merely symbolic gesture, however admirable, is not sufficient. The strength of this story, in a real sense the true conclusion to *Go Down, Moses*, as it is to the life story of Isaac McCaslin, lies primarily in Faulkner's relentless honesty in portraying the final days of a well-meaning but pathetically inadequate old man lamenting the human ruthlessness that had violated his land and his people.

The Placing
Of "Go Down, Moses"

THE PLACING
OF "GO DOWN, MOSES"

GO DOWN, MOSES does not end with the not-quite-hopeless old man of "Delta Autumn." Instead Faulkner decided to conclude his book with a story which he revised scarcely at all concerning Gavin Stevens and two old women, black and white, who were presented in a mode notably different from that of "Delta Autumn."

"Go Down, Moses," the story which provided the title for the book as a whole, begins with a description of the convicted murderer of a Chicago policeman on the day of his execution. "The face was black, smooth, impenetrable; the eyes had seen too much." To a census-taker the killer declares his birthplace to be in the country near Jefferson, Mississippi, his name to be Samuel Worsham Beauchamp, the grandmother who raised him to be Molly[1] Worsham Beauchamp. Asked for his occupation, he declares, "Getting rich too fast."

After the brief opening scene of census-taking in the penitentiary, the story is concerned with the efforts of Molly and Miss Worsham to provide a proper burial for the erring grandson, Butch. Molly's parents had been slaves of the grandfather of Miss Worsham

—whose name was changed to Habersham[2] in *Intruder in the Dust*—
and the two women had, according to Miss Worsham, grown up
"together as sisters would." The county attorney, Gavin Stevens, who
had been used briefly as a commentator in *Light in August*, who had
become prominent in the detective stories later collected in *Knight's
Gambit*, and who was to be a ubiquitous figure in Faulkner's novels
of the late forties and fifties, is used as a central consciousness
through whom the events are conveyed to the reader. Stevens is
described as having "a thin, intelligent, unstable face." He uses his
business as a hobby, having as his "serious vocation" the quixotic
project, unfinished after twenty-two years, of translating "the Old
Testament back into Classic Greek." Although he calls blacks
"darkies" and displays a notably obtuse masculine misunderstanding
of Molly's feelings about her dead grandson, Stevens raises from
the newspaper editor and other benevolent whites about the town
square, from "merchant and clerk, proprietor and employee, doctor
dentist lawyer and barber," the money necessary for the coffin,
flowers, and hearse. And as in *Light in August*—despite Faulkner's
now more ambivalent attitude toward him and much more dramatic presentation of him—Stevens acts as moral interpreter of the
action.[3] In this role he assesses Molly's feelings at the end of the
story and concludes, "*It doesn't matter to her now. Since it had to
be and she couldn't stop it, and now that it's all over and done and
finished, she doesn't care how he died. She just wanted him home,
but she wanted him to come home right.*"

In the only moment of real intensity in this story of charmingly
benevolent whites and an all but comic old black woman who wants
to be sure that it's "all in de paper," Stevens becomes, as had Isaac
McCaslin in his discussion in the commissary with Cass, the conscience of the white South. This occurs when he visits Molly and her
brother Hamp and his wife at Miss Worsham's, hoping to comfort
the old black woman in her mourning. Stevens is greeted by Hamp
but ignored by Molly, who sits close by the hearth, the fire burning
even in July, rocking and chanting of her Benjamin[4], sold to Pharaoh
in Egypt by Roth Edmonds. In trying to explain that Roth—who had
driven the youth off his place at nineteen for breaking into the commissary store—hadn't really been responsible for selling her grandson into bondage, Stevens becomes aware that Molly cannot hear

him, that she has not ever even looked at him, that he cannot explain anything to her. As Molly, then Hamp, and finally Hamp's wife join in the chanting, "Sold him in Egypt and now he dead," Stevens comprehends the futility of a white lawyer's trying to justify Roth Edmonds's action to blacks, and he rushes abruptly and desperately from the house, seeking the outside where he thinks "there will be air, space, breath."

Gavin Stevens's flight in shock from the horror of his awareness of his and Roth Edmonds's responsibility for a life like Butch Beauchamp's, and from his dismay at the difficulty—even the impossibility—of really communicating with a black, is uncharacteristic of the story. Typical of the general tenor of the presentation of black-white relationships in "Go Down, Moses" is Miss Worsham's coming to the door, trying to make Stevens feel easier about his rude departure by telling him, "It's all right. . . . It's our grief." The general sentimentalization of interracial relationships in the story as a whole and the obscurity in Faulkner's presentation of what takes place in Stevens's mind—most readers have, I think, failed to understand the episode—prevent Stevens's despairing escape from the scene of mourning from having a really substantial impact on readers of "Go Down, Moses."

Like certain things[5] in the typescripts of the stories about Lucas and Molly which ultimately become "The Fire and the Hearth," the incident seems out of keeping with the story of which it is a part; and, like those things, it provided the germ of important matters in the completed book. Faulkner seems to have conceived Stevens's hurried retreat from Molly's grief without being at that time fully conscious of its implications. It is very likely that this episode led to Faulkner's conception of a unified volume of stories concerned ultimately with Lucas and Molly, with Isaac and Cass, with old Carothers and Roth, with the hunts for deer and the bear in the disappearing wilderness and with the lives of blacks in the Egypt of the land tamed by whites.

The likelihood that "Go Down, Moses" was the source of the idea for a book of related stories is one possible explanation of Faulkner's use of the title of this story for the book as a whole. We know that Faulkner was working on "Go Down, Moses" in July 1940 along with "Was," another story primarily comic in mode which serves with it to frame the more forceful and tragic episodes in the book. It is most probable that Faulkner had by then completed the original versions of the three chapters of "The Fire and the Hearth." Only in the third does Molly become a significant character. It is unlikely but not impossible that the earliest forms of "Delta Autumn" and "The Bear" also preceded "Go Down, Moses." In any case, at some time in late 1940 or early 1941 Faulkner must suddenly have sensed the possibilities of the theme latent in Molly's chant for her lost grandson which had caused Gavin Stevens's desperate flight. Then he must have become aware of the importance of his introduction into the wilderness world of the white hunters of another black victim of Pharaoh, the unnamed mistress of Don Boyd in the magazine version of "Delta Autumn." That girl suggested a means of bringing together in a single unified volume the stories of blacks, centering on the family of Lucas Beauchamp, and the stories of hunting, ultimately centering on Isaac McCaslin, with which Faulkner had been primarily concerned since completing *The Hamlet*. She, rather than Butch Beauchamp, provided the stimulus to the great act of imagination which joined to the earlier version of "The Bear" the principal episodes of "Lion," transforming an idyll of a boy's apprenticeship to virtue in the woods into a richly complex presentation of life and death, good and evil, human aspirations and human limitations in the final version of "The Bear." In that story Carothers, the first name of the white man Molly accused of selling her Benjamin into Egypt, is given to Carothers McCaslin, the entire family's ruthless founder, who cared little for the feelings of either his mistress or his daughter. And when Faulkner revised "Delta Autumn" to link it more completely to the tragic history of the McCaslin family, he transferred the girl, the "doe," from Don Boyd to Carothers Edmonds, making her a victim of the twentieth-century inheritor of McCaslin land and responsibility, a victim to be paired in the reader's mind with that very different victim of white power, her cousin Butch Beauchamp.

Faulkner's decision to place "Go Down, Moses" after "Delta Autumn," to give it the emphasis which resulted from such placing, probably reflects its role in the genesis of the imaginative process by which he linked together the discordant parts of the book that bears the story's name. And it probably reflects, as well, a distaste

he felt at this point in his life for concluding a book with an ending
as gloomy as that of "Delta Autumn." He was to go on to works such
as *A Fable, Intruder in the Dust,* and *Requiem for a Nun* and was
to deliver not many years later a celebrated speech expounding
man's ability to prevail. Placing this, the fourth of the stories concerned with the Beauchamp descendants of Carothers McCaslin
and containing a symbolic hearth fire, at the end of the book instead
of immediately after "The Fire and the Hearth" strengthened the
coherence of *Go Down, Moses* by causing it to conclude with two
modern black victims of Carothers Edmonds's callousness, one
facing down old Isaac McCaslin in the shrunken woods of the delta
and the other mourned by Molly, the aged wife of Lucas Beauchamp. "Old Luke Beauchamp" is mentioned only once in "Go
Down, Moses," as a man who is known to have money in the bank
and who is therefore a potential contributor to the funeral expenses
of Butch; but a careful reader attuned to the genealogical relationships of the McCaslins will recall that Butch and the unnamed girl
are third cousins, black inheritors of money from the will of
Carothers McCaslin, grandchildren of Lucas and of the lost Tennie's
Jim who had rejected his legacy and fled from the Edmonds place
on the day he came of age.

Another and an important reason for Faulkner's selecting "Go
Down, Moses" for the concluding story of the book and for giving
its title to the entire work is the theme of redemption implicit in its
reference to the Negro spiritual. In the story Molly sings only in
grief for her grandson sold into Egypt by Carothers Edmonds and
now dead. Were it not for its lighter tone and more superficial
characterization, "Go Down, Moses" might be as pessimistic a story
as "Delta Autumn." Butch's fate is even less hopeful than that of
the girl betrayed by her love for Roth. But the well-known spiritual
improvised on by Molly, Hamp, and Hamp's wife, and alluded to in
the title of the story and of the book serves to suggest a hopeful
perspective and to underscore religious themes sounded in earlier
stories. Like the New England Puritans, the southern slaves used
biblical narratives metaphorically to describe their own condition.
Just as in the seventeenth century, William Bradford thought of
Moses viewing the Promised Land from the top of Mount Pisgah
when writing of the storm-tossed Pilgrims huddled together against

a Massachusetts December, the anonymous composers of the spiritual "Go Down, Moses" referred to their own bondage in slavery when they spoke of the people of Israel in Egypt's land. I feel sure that Faulkner expected his readers to remember the conclusion of the spiritual and wished to suggest to them the blacks' ultimate redemption from servitude. It might not be, as old Isaac had suggested in "Delta Autumn," for "a thousand or two thousand years in America," but it would come. Till then blacks like Molly and Lucas, Butch Beauchamp and Tennie's Jim's granddaughter, Rider and old Sam Fathers would have to endure being blacks in America. But ultimately freedom would come, as the spiritual promises:

> As Israel stood by the water side,
>   Let my people go.
> By God's command it did divide,
>   Let my people go.
>
> When they reached the other shore,
>   Let my people go.
> They sang a song of triumph o'er,
>   Let my people go.

The spiritual "Go Down, Moses" is clearly related to the theme of freedom recurring in the fourth section of "The Bear," a theme which manifests itself most nobly in young Isaac McCaslin's deluded dream of acting as the redeemer of his land from the curse of evil and slavery. The spiritual also serves to reinforce a theme of redemption from evil, which is present in the stories of "The Fire and the Hearth," but which is understated and is apt to be missed by a reader distracted by the comic tone of the stories and by Faulkner's later interpolations dealing with calamitous episodes in the boyhood of Roth and the young manhood of Lucas. This theme is reflected in both the original and the second title of the oldest preserved typescript of the third story, "An Absolution" and "Apotheosis." It was reinforced by a passage Faulkner added in revising the first story for book publication, the passage describing Lucas's finding the single gold coin, which provoked him into the foolish hunt for buried treasure that almost destroyed his marriage. The passage, already quoted in chapter 3, concerns the blow on his face of the chunk of earthenware vessel containing the coin as "a sort of final admonitory pat from the spirit of darkness and solitude, the old earth, perhaps the old ancestors themselves." Here the old ancestors are clearly different from those moral and benevolent forebears of Sam Fathers who were celebrated in "The Old People," and the "final admonitory pat" led to Lucas's reckless and selfish pursuit of wealth.

In the third story Molly, in telling Roth that she must have a divorce, reveals to him that Lucas is doing something that "the Lord aint meant for folks to do," that Lucas does not even get out of bed to go to church anymore, and that her greatest fear is that he will find some money. Even the white man, Roth, comes finally to understand her: "The curse of God. . . . What it might do to him, even to a man sixty-seven years old, who had . . . three times that sum in a Jefferson bank; even a thousand dollars on which there was no sweat, at least none of his own. And to George, the daughter's husband, who had not a dollar anywhere, who was not yet twenty-five and with an eighteen-year-old wife expecting a child next spring." At the conclusion of the story, after he has called off the divorce proceedings and restored marital peace to his family, Lucas forces the metal-detecting machine on Roth (who would have been willing to allow a little part-time prospecting that Molly did not know about), telling him that he wants it "clean off this place." Absolved from the curse of pride and selfishness, Lucas does not want to be subject to further temptation. In conclusion he declares, "Man has got three score and ten years on this earth, the Book says. He can want a heap in that time and a heap of what he can want is due to come to him, if he just starts soon enough. I done waited too late to start. . . . I am near to the end of my three score and ten, and I reckon to find that money aint for me."

Faulkner's choice of "Go Down, Moses" for the concluding story of his book is easy to understand. Paired with "Was," it framed in lighter tones the central episodes of the volume. It carried the unhappy history of Carothers McCaslin's descendants down to 1940 and out of the archaic wilderness into the biracial society of a twentieth-century southern town. And, pleasing to a man concurrently engaged in writing pleasant patriotic stories about noble and courageous country people for *The Saturday Evening Post* and soon to

immerse himself in protracted labors on *A Fable,* it suggested
through the Negro spiritual that provided its title a hopeful Christian
perspective on the discouraging events that comprised the latter
portion of the book.

Despite its thematic appropriateness, "Go Down, Moses" is not
a wholly satisfactory conclusion to the book. It is one thing to open
the book with a comic prelude presenting a boy's view of slaveholding society in 1859 and quite another to end it, after the inclu-
sion of "The Bear" and "Delta Autumn," with a story that presents,
even somewhat comically, the efforts of an aged black woman to
bury her criminal grandson. After the tragic story of Isaac McCaslin,
"Go Down, Moses" seems too easy in its final assertion of the value
of Molly's bringing Butch "home right." It seems to undercut the
seriousness of the book as a whole. The conclusion lacks the essential appropriateness of the endings of Faulkner's great early novels:
of Ben Compson subsiding into serene silence, grasping his broken
flower as the surrey reverses direction and circles the monument in
the accustomed way; of Anse introducing to his remaining family
the new Mrs. Bundren, of Quentin Compson insistently declaring
that he doesn't hate the South; or even of Lena Grove announcing
as she enters Tennessee, "My, my. A body does get around."

The principal cause of dissatisfaction with "Go Down, Moses"
is Faulkner's sentimental presentation of black-white relationships.
The too charming portrait of a southern community[6] is particularly
disturbing to readers who have just experienced the immensely
poignant and entirely convincing scene between old Isaac and
Tennie's Jim's granddaughter, a scene created through an entirely
different degree of imaginative involvement from that responsible
for the creation of "Go Down, Moses." In the concluding story the
white people are much too kindly to be entirely convincing human
beings. The fat old editor readily agrees to contribute a major share
of the burial expenses of a black murderer for the novelty of it, declaring, "It will be the first time in my life I ever paid money for
copy I had already promised before hand I wont print." In marked
contrast to the grudging fifteen-minute closing actually observed by
the merchants of Oxford for Faulkner's own funeral, the fictitious
merchants of Jefferson willingly hand over to Gavin Stevens their
dollar, half-dollar, or quarter contributions to the expenses for

Butch's burial. A large delegation composed of "Negroes and whites both" greets the train carrying the body back to Mississippi from Illinois. Miss Worsham, her relationship with Molly apparently never troubled by any altercation such as those which estranged Roth and Henry, Lucas and Zack, is able to speak to Stevens quite naturally of "our grief."

If the whites in "Go Down, Moses" are implausibly charming and indulgent of the vagaries of the "darkies," Molly, the black woman, is not quite credible either as a human being. Faulkner's blacks, distinct from his characters with mixed blood such as Joe Christmas, Charles Bon, and Lucas and James Beauchamp, often are uncomfortably close to conventional white stereotypes. A number of them are variations on Aunt Jemima and Uncle Remus. Dilsey of *The Sound and the Fury*, about whom Faulkner could write in 1945 simply, "They endured"; the Lucas Beauchamp of *Intruder in the Dust* and the Nancy Mannigoe, "nigger," murderer, dope-fiend, whore, and nun of *Requiem for a Nun*, are conceived in such idealized terms that they seem both more and less than human. In Faulkner stories they are without ordinary human weaknesses, and therefore their lives have no moral drama. Molly is neither a super-human monument of strength like Dilsey or the Lucas of *Intruder in the Dust* nor an agent of redemption like Nancy, but she is only somewhat more credible than they. She seems to have been conceived largely for contrast and for comedy, to be almost a caricature rather than a believable human being. This is more troubling in "Go Down, Moses" than it had been in the essentially comic stories of "The Fire and the Hearth." In a final comic twist which pretty much erases any serious effect her mourning has had on the reader, she insists in heavy dialect that instead of being protected from publicity, as Gavin Stevens and the editor assumed she desired, she wants a full account in the paper of Butch's reception in Jefferson and burial, "all of hit."

To be sure Molly is presented externally as she is perceived by Gavin Stevens, and Faulkner has dramatized Gavin's view to distinguish it from his own. But in this story, as elsewhere in Faulkner's work before *The Town*, it is difficult to regard Stevens's attitude as entirely distinct from Faulkner's own, and Stevens's admiring yet patronizing idea of Molly Beauchamp seems to reflect a conception

of blacks sometimes evident in Stevens's creator. It is disconcerting
to be given even a taste of complacent white superiority toward
blacks in the final pages of a book dedicated to Caroline Barr, the
prototype in life of Molly, a book which in the fourth section of "The
Bear" included the following ledger entries concerning Eunice's
drowning:

> [Buddy] *June 21th 1833 Drownd herself*
> [Buck]   *23 Jun 1833 Who in hell ever heard of*
>   *a niger drownding him self . . .*
> [Buddy] unhurried, with complete finality,
>   *Aug 13th 1833 Drownd herself.*

Go Down, Moses is a transitional book. In it, despite remarkable
feats of imaginative synthesis, Faulkner failed to achieve the free,
organic wholeness he had secured in *Absalom, Absalom!* and even,
two years before *Go Down, Moses*, in *The Hamlet*. And the student
of Faulkner's writings can detect in this volume, the only one he
published between the attack on Pearl Harbor and 1948, signs of
developments in his thinking and writing which would become fully
apparent in the later works. Particularly noticeable are the indica-
tions of increasing optimism, idealization, and sentimentality in the
concluding story and of wordy abstract theorizing, lengthy talk
about North and South, the nature of men and God, and belief and
endurance, in the conversation in the commissary between Ike and
Cass in "The Bear." But if *Go Down, Moses* contains foreshadowings
of tendencies which weakened Faulkner's subsequent novels, it also
contains many things equal, and sometimes even superior, to anything in the great early works. Among these is the fine comic tale,
"Was," a boy's view of slavery and a wonderfully apt prelude to the
book. Especially memorable are the great moments of tragic awareness—Roth's realizing what he had done to Henry and its consequences, Isaac's coming into his family heritage in reading the
ledgers at sixteen, and the latter's final, bitter recognition of his
limitations—in "Delta Autumn." Faulkner's prose never surpassed
the somber power displayed in the descriptions of Ike's experience
of the wilderness in the first and last sections of "The Bear." A particularly distinguishing triumph of *Go Down, Moses* among Faulkner's works is its delicate balancing of affirmation and resignation

in that fifth section of "The Bear," when eighteen-year-old Isaac McCaslin, in the midst of the immortal summer woods, salutes as "grandfather" the snake symbolic of all knowledge, of pariah-hood, and of death. A similar justness of balance is maintained in the introductory paragraphs describing Isaac McCaslin, which Faulkner placed before the opening story, "Was," in an effort to pull the stories together for book publication. In these paragraphs which are read first, but which were probably written last, Faulkner informs us of the widespread opinion that Isaac was done out of his inheritance by his cousin, but we are told that Isaac did not share that opinion. We are given a sympathetic account of his refusal to own any property except the iron cot and the thin mattress he used in the woods. Both the virtue and the defeat of the man are contained—and for the innocent first reader, concealed—in the last phrase of the first paragraph: "uncle to half a county and father to no one."

Appendixes

A GENEALOGY FOR *GO DOWN, MOSES*

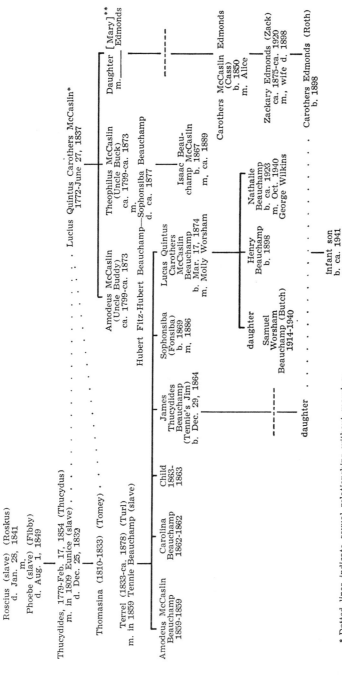

* Dotted lines indicate sexual relationships without marriage.
** Mary McCaslin Edmonds is never identified by name in Go Down, Moses. She is named in a genealogical chart in the Alderman Library. See above, p. 33.

THE NEGRO SPIRITUAL
"GO DOWN, MOSES"

When Israel was in Egypt's land,
  Let my people go.
Oppressed so hard they could not stand,
  Let my people go.

We need not always weep and mourn,
  Let my people go.
And wear these slav'ry chains forlorn,
  Let my people go.

The devil thought he had us fast,
  Let my people go.
But we thought we'd break his chains at last,
  Let my people go.

Thus saith the Lord, bold Moses said,
  Let my people go.
If not I'll smite your first-born dead,

Let my people go.

No more shall they in bondage toil,
    Let my people go.
Let them come out with Egypt's spoil,
    Let my people go.

When Israel out of Egypt came,
    Let my people go.
And left the proud oppressive land,
    Let my people go.

O 'twas a dark and dismal night,
    Let my people go.
When Moses led the Israelites,
    Let my people go.

The Lord told Moses what to do,
    Let my people go.
To lead the children of Israel thro',
    Let my people go.

As Israel stood by the water side,
    Let my people go.
By God's command it did divide,
    Let my people go.

When they reached the other shore,
    Let my people go.
They sang a song of triumph o'er,
    Let my people go.

(Chorus)

Go down, Moses,
'Way down in Egypt's land.
Tell ole Pharaoh,
Let my people go.

NOTES

CHAPTER ONE

1. "And Other Stories" was dropped from the title at Faulkner's request after the first printing. Michael Millgate believes that the original title may have been an editor's rather than Faulkner's. *The Achievement of William Faulkner* (New York: Random House, 1966), pp. 202-3, 328.

2. On May 8, 1958, Faulkner told a class at the University of Virginia that if he had been consulted about including the fourth section when the story was published by itself, he would have said, "Take this out, this doesn't belong in this as a short story, it's part of the novel but not part of the story." Frederick L. Gwynn and Joseph L. Blotner, eds., *Faulkner in the University* (Charlottesville: University of Virginia Press, 1959), p. 273.

3. In Nagano, Japan, Faulkner said that he was able to write *The Sound and the Fury* without any dependence on notes. *As I Lay Dying* took only six or seven weeks to write and, Faulkner stated, was fully conceived before he put pen to paper.

4. Major de Spain's hunting camp was modeled on one in the Talla-hatchie River bottom near Batesville in Panola County, Mississippi, bordering on Lafayette County to the west, where an annual deer hunt was staged by General James Stone—lawyer, bank president, rival of Faulkner's grandfather J. W. T. Falkner, and father of Faulkner's friend and mentor Phil Stone. The camp was only 30 miles from Oxford, but the trip by rail extended almost 150 miles. The last portion of the trip was over a line built by a lumber company after General Stone had sold much of his neighboring timberlands. Ash,

who was called Ad in "Lion" and given a son and a surname, Wylie, in the version of "A Bear Hunt" published in *Big Woods*, was patterned after Ad, or Add, Bush, a former slave who was cook for the hunting party headed by Dr. A. C. Bramlett and/or that headed by General Stone (accounts vary). John B. Cullen in collaboration with Floyd C. Watkins, *Old Times in the Faulkner Country* (Chapel Hill: University of North Carolina Press, 1961), pp. 27, 29-30; John Faulkner, *My Brother Bill* (New York: Trident Press, 1963), pp. 156-58; William Evans Stone V, "Our Cotehouse" in James W. Webb and A. Wigfall Green, eds., *William Faulkner of Oxford* (Baton Rouge: Louisiana State University Press, 1965), pp. 81-82.

5. In *My Brother Bill* John Faulkner tells of William's borrowing, at approximately this time, plots for two stories from unpublished pieces of his (pp. 206-7). It is possible that "A Point of Law" and "Gold Is Not Always" are the stories. But it is risky to rely completely on the often erratic memory of John Faulkner.

6. A photograph of this page is included in James B. Meriwether's *The Literary Career of William Faulkner* (Princeton: Princeton University Press, 1961), fig. 17. Faulkner was inconsistent in spelling Molly's name even in *Go Down, Moses*. It ends in *y* in "The Fire and the Hearth," but in the final story, "Go Down, Moses," it terminates still in *ie*. I have used *Molly* in all cases here, except in direct quotations.

7. John Faulkner mentions a great-grandchild of Caroline Barr named Molly. *My Brother Bill*, p. 51.

8. Ibid., p. 215.

9. *Ibid.*, p. 51.

10. See William Faulkner, *Essays, Speeches, and Public Letters*, ed. James B. Meriwether (New York: Random House, 1965), pp. 117-18.

11. Clifton Bondurant Webb, "Swing Low for Sweet Callie" in Webb and Green, *Faulkner of Oxford*, p. 127.

12. This passage is contained in the typescript of "A Point of Law," pp. 14-15, in the Alderman Library, but it did not appear in the version of the story published in *Collier's*. In slightly revised form the passage was put back into the story in *Go Down, Moses*, and two related passages were added in other places (pp. 71, 108, 118). All American editions of *Go Down, Moses* follow the pagination of the first edition.

CHAPTER TWO

1. Faulkner once told Malcolm Cowley rather casually that, of course, Rider was one of the McCaslin Negroes. Malcolm Cowley, *The Faulkner-Cowley File* (New York: Viking Press, 1966), p. 113.

2. Faulkner attempted to resolve some of the discrepancies in rewriting "A Bear Hunt" for *Big Woods*.

3. Sam was first given his name in "A Justice." An Indian called Had-Two-Fathers had been mentioned once, casually without any explanation, in "Red Leaves." He was removed from the text of the story used for *The Portable Faulkner* but appears in the *Collected Stories*.

4. Ellen Sutpen's occupation probably suggested to Faulkner the role he gave Molly in these passages.

5. See John Faulkner, *My Brother Bill*, p. 48.

6. For an account of several discarded pages from early typescripts of "Was" and "Go Down, Moses" presented by Faulkner to Don Brennan in July 1940, see Russell Roth, "The Brennan Papers: Faulkner in Manuscript," *Perspective* 2 (Summer 1949): 219-24.

7. The outcome of the poker game in "Was" is an elaboration of an anecdote told of the card-playing law-school days of Eustace Graham, the district attorney who prosecuted Lee Goodwin in *Sanctuary*. Left alone at the end of a game with Graham, the proprietor of the livery stable asks, "How many cards did you draw, Eustace?" He is told, "Three, Mr. Harris." "Hmmm. Who dealt the cards, Eustace?" he asks. "I did, Mr. Harris," Graham responds. "I pass, Eustace."

8. Primitives rendered from the outside like Dilsey and Lena Grove have no inner lives which are accessible to the reader. That of V. K. Ratliff is rendered with little imaginative intensity.

9. In the final version of the story published in *Go Down, Moses*, Isaac McCaslin had a wife but no children.

10. Renamed Carothers Edmonds in *Go Down, Moses*.

CHAPTER THREE

1. Here Faulkner transforms Virgil and Euripides. Priam was killed during the sack of Troy (recall the player's speech about Pyrrhus in *Hamlet*). Hecuba survived to be carried away toward Greece and, ultimately, to be turned, in Ovid's *Metamorphoses*, into a bitch.

2. In *My Brother Bill* John Faulkner tells of his father's buying the children two beagle hounds and of William's going hunting and accidentally killing one of the dogs. "He dropped his gun and forgot it and brought the dog home in his arms. When he got there he laid the little dog on the porch and went to his room and locked himself in and cried. He was about fourteen then, I think, and did not take up another gun until he was grown and went on the deer hunt below Batesville" (p. 92).

CHAPTER FOUR

1. Only on page seven of *Go Down, Moses* is McCaslin Edmonds given his full three-word name.

2. See the genealogy, Appendix A.

3. See the genealogy, Appendix A.

4. According to John Faulkner, this was based on an actual trip William took with "Mr. Buster Callicot." *My Brother Bill* (New York: Trident Press, 1963), p. 92.

5. "Lion" was set approximately in the late nineteen-twenties or early thirties. The Dempsey-Tunney fight was referred to, and Boon's use of a suitcase to carry the whiskey suggests prohibition was in force.

CHAPTER FIVE

1. In the Alderman Library a page of the setting typescript of *Go Down, Moses* numbered "206bis," which contains material from the latter portion of the first section of "The Bear," carries the notation "Rec'd 9/9 41." Presumably the first portion of section one was received before that date in September 1941, and the story as a whole was finished in a preliminary form still earlier.

2. See above, p. 33.

3. In a memorial essay, "William Faulkner 1897-1962," Tate wrote, "Years ago, when I was editing *The Sewanee Review,* I had some correspondence with him; his letters were signed 'Faulkner,' I wrote him that English nobility followed this practice and I never heard from him again." *Sewanee Review* (Winter 1963), p. 160.

4. On p. 4 of *Go Down, Moses* Faulkner writes of Isaac's "cousin McCaslin" born in 1850 and sixteen years his senior, although on p. 273 he gives 1867 as Ike's birthdate.

5. *Life,* March 5, 1956, pp. 51-52; included in William Faulkner, *Essays, Speeches, and Public Letters,* ed. James B. Meriwether (New York: Random House, 1965), pp. 86-91.

6. As late as July 24, 1948, Faulkner, in making a humorous document commissioning the *Minmargary,* a houseboat he and some friends built to use on the Sardis Reservoir, invoked the authority he might have inherited from his "Great grandfather William C. Falkner Colonel (Paroled) Second Mississippi Infantry Provisional Army Confederate States of America." He named the *Minmargary* "A Ship of the Line in the Provisional Navy of the Confederate States of America" and signed himself "William C. Falkner II"; see James W. Webb and A. Wigfall Green, eds., *William Faulkner of Oxford* (Baton Rouge: Louisiana State University Press, 1965), appendix, p. 234.

7. Isaac's ideas were also anticipated by Lonnie Grinnup, a descendent of Louis Grenier (one of the original settlers of Yoknapatawpha County), who in "Hand upon the Waters" lived in a hut and fished at the center of the more than a thousand acres his ancestors had owned without knowing it was his family's land. And Gavin Stevens "believed he would not have cared, would have declined to accept the idea that any one man could or should own that much of the earth which belongs to all." William Faulkner, *Knight's Gambit* (New York: Random House, 1949), p. 66. "Hand upon the Waters" was first published in the *Saturday Evening Post,* November 4, 1939.

8. Caroline Barr's fifth husband took her to Arkansas and mistreated her there. Faulkner's father sent a Mr. Bennett, who brought her back to Oxford. John Faulkner, *My Brother Bill,* p. 49.

9. This discussion was slightly trimmed for the revised version, but all its essential features were retained.

10. Only on the IOUs written by Uncle Hubert is Ike's full name, Isaac Beauchamp McCaslin, disclosed. *Go Down, Moses,* p. 307.

CHAPTER SIX

1. Changes in the pagination of "Delta Autumn" in the setting typescript of *Go Down, Moses,* which is in the Alderman Library, suggest that Faulkner once intended to place "Delta Autumn" before "The Bear."

2. Jean-Paul Sartre, "Time in Faulkner: The Sound and the Fury," translated by Martine Darmon with the assistance of the editors, in Frederick J. Hoffman and Olga W. Vickery, *William Faulkner: Three Decades of Criticism* (Lansing: Michigan State University Press, 1960), pp. 225-32.

3. In an interview with Jean Stein, Faulkner defended his practice of moving his characters about in time as well as in space by arguing that "time is a fluid condition which has no existence except in the momentary avatars

of individual people. There is no such thing as *was*—only *is*. If *was* existed, there would be no grief or sorrow." Malcolm Cowley, ed., *Writers at Work: The Paris Review Interviews*, 1st series (New York: Compass Books, 1959), p. 141.

4. Bramlett Roberts, son of Faulkner's hunting companion, Ike Roberts, tells of the novelist's reminiscing about a man named Westmoreland. "He—Westmoreland—had a single barrel, rickety shotgun. It was pieced together with baling wire. Bill heard some shooting over in a clearing and when he got in sight he saw a large oak tree with no other trees around it and the squirrels were playing all over the tree. Wes had shot his gun. When it fired the barrel came off: the stock went one way, the barrel another; and the forearm another. Bill went up and was going to kill some of the squirrels; it was full of squirrels. And Wes said, 'Oh no, don't bother 'em, don't bother 'em! They're mine!'" Webb and Green, *William Faulkner of Oxford*, pp. 151-52. A variation on this episode appears close to the end of *The Hamlet* when Henry Armstid drives Ratliff, who is trying to explain Flem Snopes's trickery, away from the pit in which he was digging for buried gold. "Get out of my hole," he tells Ratliff. "Get outen it."

5. According to John B. Cullen, General Stone sold much of his land shortly before 1915. "Old Colonel Stone owned a good bit of land, the place where he built his camp and the Porter farm, four or five hundred acres with timber on it. He let the Porter farm go rather than pay his drainage tax on it. The Carrier Lumber Company or Lamb Fish, a big-time lumberman, cut the timber and sold the land to people who started farming. In 1915 and 1916 near Charleston, Mississippi, there were miles of lumber in stacks high as a man could make them." John B. Cullen and Floyd C. Watkins, *Old Times in the Faulkner Country* (Chapel Hill: University of North Carolina Press, 1961), pp. 29-30.

6. *My Brother Bill*, p. 92.

CHAPTER SEVEN

1. One of the six, "Delta Autumn," was published at approximately the same time as the book.

2. Although Faulkner made Sam's mother a quadroon, he was so conscious of Sam's Negro blood that he got the racial proportions curiously confused.

3. Russell Roth, "The Brennan Papers: Faulkner in Manuscript," *Perspective* 2 (Summer 1949): 219-24.

CHAPTER EIGHT

1. *Go Down, Moses*, p. 54.

2. Ibid., p. 58.

3. Ibid., p. 109.

4. Ibid., p. 106. This description of Isaac seems related to the "inviolable and immortal adolescence" of Hubert Beauchamp which Faulkner stressed in describing the burlap-covered legacy, pp. 303-6.

5. "The Art of Fiction: An Interview with William Faulkner," *Accent* (Summer 1956), p. 175.

6. In a class at the University of Virginia on April 24, 1958. Frederick

L. Gwynn and Joseph L. Blotner, eds., *Faulkner in the University* (Charlottesville: University of Virginia Press, 1959), p. 246.

7. In class, March 11, 1957. Ibid., p. 54.

8. One typescript page numbered 237 is in the Alderman Library. It corresponds roughly to material on pages 236-37 of *Go Down, Moses*.

9. *Go Down, Moses*, pp. 104-9. There are a number of discrepancies within this passage, and a few pages later there are three odd genealogical references which agree neither with the final genealogical scheme of "The Bear" nor with each other. On p. 114 Isaac McCaslin is referred to as Roth Edmonds's uncle, and Roth speaks to his father about "our grandmother McCaslin" being as close in blood to old Carothers as Uncle Buck and Uncle Buddy. On p. 116 Isaac McCaslin's financial dependence on the Edmonds family is carried into the third generation; he is described as "living on the doled pittance which his great-nephew now in his turn sent him each month." Roth, who, except in the reference on p. 114, is never in *Go Down, Moses* more than a fifth cousin to Isaac, is described later on p. 116 as taking over the management and running it insofar as he could "as his father and grandfather and great-grandfather had done before him." On p. 71 Roth had been identified as the great-grandson of Carothers McCaslin, but it is impossible to reconcile any genealogical scheme which put him in a direct line of inheritance with the scene in the commissary where Isaac renounces his heritage to Roth's grandfather, McCaslin Edmonds.

Another discrepancy concerns the relationship of Lucas's birth to the deaths of Buck and Buddy. On p. 39 of "The Fire and the Hearth" Faulkner writes of Lucas's remembering "Old Buck and Buddy in the living flesh," and on p. 114 Zack Edmonds speaks of Lucas's being "old enough even to remember Uncle Buck and Uncle Buddy a little," but on p. 36 Lucas is described as merely "almost . . . coeval" with the twin brothers, and in "The Bear," on p. 274, Faulkner writes that when Lucas was born, the twins "had been dead inside the same twelve-months almost five years."

Still another discrepancy concerns the ownership of the bungalow Isaac inhabited in Jefferson, which was described in the fourth section of "The Bear" as being built by Isaac and his partner of materials furnished and on land owned by his wife's father, so it was a "dowery from one" and a "wedding-present from three." In "Delta Autumn" Isaac is described simply as being, after his wife's death, the bungalow's owner (pp. 351-52); but in the passage inserted before "Was" (pp. 3-4) as general introduction to all of *Go Down, Moses*, Faulkner wrote that the house had been willed him by his wife but that he had only pretended to accept it to make her dying easy, and it "was not his, will or not, chancery dying wishes mortmain possession or whatever, himself merely holding it for his wife's sister and her children who had lived in it with him since his wife's death, holding himself welcome to live in one room of it as he had during his wife's time." This final definition of Isaac McCaslin's relationship to real estate he had once helped to build as a wedding present for his wife seems to be an elaboration of an intermediate version which appears in "The Fire and the Hearth," on p. 106, where Isaac is described as "living in his dead wife's house the title to which he . . . declined to assume" but where no mention is made of his wife's sister.

10. *Go Down, Moses*, pp. 105, 273.

11. Still another version of the legacy appears in "The Fire and the Hearth" on p. 126, where Lucas tells Roth that he has "them three thousand dollars old Carothers left me, right there in that bank yonder."

12. *Go Down, Moses*, pp. 273, 276, 281, 308-10.

13. Ibid., p. 306.

14. Interview with Jean Stein, in Malcolm Cowley, ed., *Writers at Work: The Paris Review Interviews*, 1st series (New York: Compass Books, 1959), pp. 128-29, 134.

15. That is, after the general pattern of the fourth section had been worked out.

16. A description of Roth's thoughts as he looked at the impenetrable face of Lucas is contained on pp. 14-15 of a typescript of "A Point of Law" in the Alderman Library. It was removed from the story before publication in *Collier's*, June 22, 1940. When he restored the description to the first chapter of "The Fire and the Hearth" in *Go Down, Moses*, Faulkner did surprisingly little to adjust it to Lucas's now mixed racial heritage. He simply had Roth think of Lucas as "a man most of whose blood was pure ten thousand years when my own anonymous beginnings became mixed enough to produce me" (p. 71) instead of thinking of him as he had in the typescript as "a man whose race was pure ten thousand years when my own anonymous beginnings . . .

17. *Go Down, Moses*, pp. 99-100.

18. As the genealogical chart for the McCaslin family in the Alderman Library suggests, Faulkner originally intended to reinforce the connection between Carothers Edmonds and his grandfather by giving them the same name. In the final text of *Go Down, Moses* this survives only in the single mention on p. 7 of the grandfather's full name, Carothers McCaslin Edmonds. After the older man had been renamed, for all practical purposes, McCaslin Edmonds, Faulkner changed the younger man's name to McCaslin also. Apparently he decided in the end that it was more important to emphasize Roth's relationship to the original McCaslin, Lucius Quintus Carothers, and changed his name back to Carothers Edmonds.

19. Faulkner at one time, oddly, gave Boyd a military background much like his own. A passage on the back of p. 4A of the typescript of "Delta Autumn" in the Alderman Library tells of Boyd's lying about his age in order to serve in 1917-18 and of his being demobilized as a pilot in the air corps. Faulkner himself was refused by the American Air Corps because of his height, not his age.

20. *Go Down, Moses*, pp. 110-16. Roth's experience, which dramatizes the ambivalence of southern feelings about Negroes, is similar to those of many white boys of Faulkner's generation and even later. Erskine Caldwell describes a comparable event from his childhood in his book on southern Negroes, *In Search of Bisco* (New York: Farrar, Straus, 1965).

21. *Go Down, Moses*, p. 118. A similar passage, also developed from a description of Roth's response to Lucas's impenetrable face, which had been in the original typescript of "The Fire and the Hearth," is attributed to the point of view of Isaac McCaslin (p. 108).

22. Concerning the discrepancy between this account and the account elsewhere in *Go Down, Moses* of the relationship between Lucas's birth and the death of the McCaslin twins, see n. 12, this chapter.

23. *Go Down, Moses*, pp. 45-59.

24. Everything about Molly and Zack's behavior in this section suggests that they were innocent, but an odd passage in the third chapter makes the matter ambiguous. In the midst of the troubles caused by Lucas's treasure hunting, Roth was on the point of telling him that Zack lay down in peace when his time came because he never "had anything about his wife in her old age to have to say God forgive me for doing that." But he stopped short and said something else (p. 121).

25. In addition to those cited in the passage which follows, see those cited above on pp. 75-76.

26. *Go Down, Moses*, p. 36. It is possible, but I do not think it likely, that Faulkner intended Lucas's judgment of Isaac to reflect his own changing state of mind, to sympathize with Isaac when he himself felt oppressed, to be scornful when he was elated.

27. *Go Down, Moses*, pp. 39-40.

CHAPTER NINE

1. A minor discrepancy, the placing of Ike's age at fourteen instead of sixteen when he discovers the secrets of his family's past (see p. 351), suggests that the revision of "Delta Autumn," like the revisions of the stories of "The Fire and the Hearth," may have preceded some final changes in "The Bear."

2. Alterations of the page numbers of the setting typescript in the Alderman Library indicate this.

3. This portion of the discourse originated in the passage lamenting the ruined delta, which Faulkner placed close to the end of the original version of "Delta Autumn" and retained in the final version.

4. This, of course, is inconsistent with the twenty-one-year-old Isaac who disputes with his cousin in the fourth section of "The Bear."

5. It may be that Faulkner's changed presentation of Isaac's wife was suggested by the passage in which Roth's mistress asked the old man if he remembered anything about love. He would have reread this passage before beginning his revisions of the story.

6. The portion of this quotation that follows the dash was added in revision.

EPILOGUE

1. In "Go Down, Moses," however, Faulkner retained the spelling he had originally used in the stories of "The Fire and the Hearth." Thus, Molly's name is spelled Mollie in the final story.

2. Both names were used in *The Unvanquished*. Dr. Worsham had been the Episcopal minister in Jefferson before the war, and the self-important busybody, Mrs. Habersham, saw to it that Colonel John Sartoris married Cousin Drusilla Hawk whose reputation she was sure he had ruined. Worsham resembles the name of a Negro blacksmith, Earl Wortham, who shod Faulkner's horses. Another name in *Go Down, Moses* may be derived from that of Chester Carruthers, driver for Faulkner's grandfather.

3. The Gavin Stevens of this story should not be confused with the rather foolish romantic bachelor of *The Town*. Here his "unstable" face suggests moral sensitivity instead of giddiness and his literary ambition, a wonderful

example of Faulkner's comic extravagance, is not essentially relevant to his role in the story.

4. Molly has confused Joseph with his brother Benjamin, the greatly loved child of Jacob's old age. Molly's lament recalls another victim sold into "Egypt" who was cared for by another old Negro woman modeled on Callie Barr.

> His name's Benjy now, Caddy said.
> How come it is, Dilsey said. He aint wore out the name
> he was born with yet, is he.
> Benjamin came out of the bible, Caddy said. It's a
> better name for him than Maury was.
> How come it is, Dilsey said.
> Mother says it is, Caddy said.
>   (from *The Sound and the Fury*)

5. Notable instances are the fire on the hearth itself, which first appeared in a story not concerned with the endurance of a marriage, and the reference to the "tragic complexity" of Roth Edmonds's "motherless childhood," which appeared before Faulkner had conceived the details of that childhood.

6. Both Cleanth Brooks in *William Faulkner: The Yoknapatawpha Country* and Arthur Mizener in "The Thin Intelligent Face of American Fiction," *Kenyon Review* (Autumn 1955) regard "Go Down, Moses" much more favorably than I do. They take seriously the idea of a southern community presented in the story. Mizener argues that "Go Down, Moses" "shows us the grandeur and pathos, the innocence and incongruity of the community's solidarity which makes Miss Worsham speak . . . unconsciously . . . of 'our grief' " (p. 517).

Gavin Stevens's perception of the futility of his efforts to break through the racial barrier in a time of tragic crisis undercuts what I regard as the sentimentalized portrayal of white benevolence in the story. But, as I have said, this is presented so obscurely that it seems unlikely that Faulkner himself was fully aware of the undercutting.

INDEX